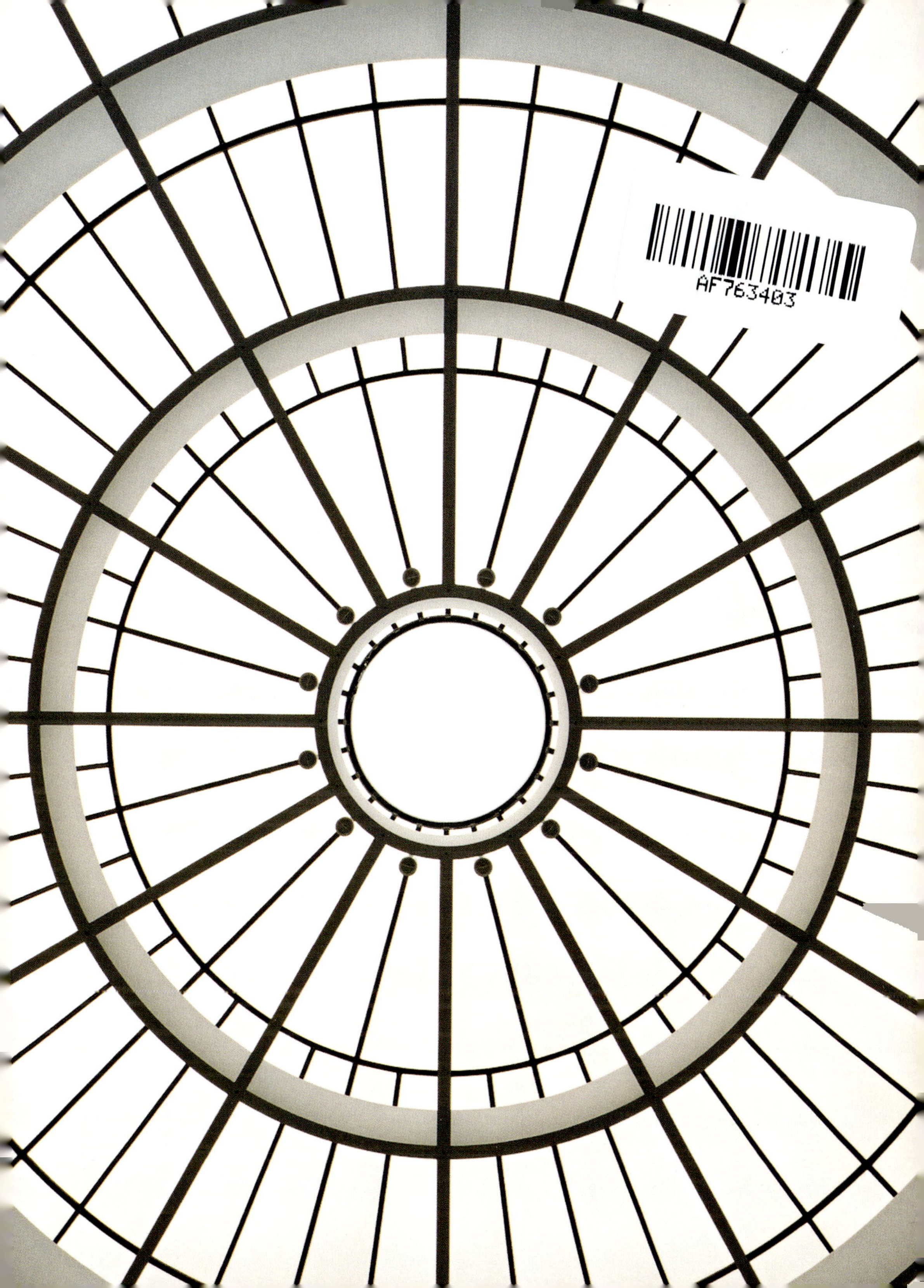

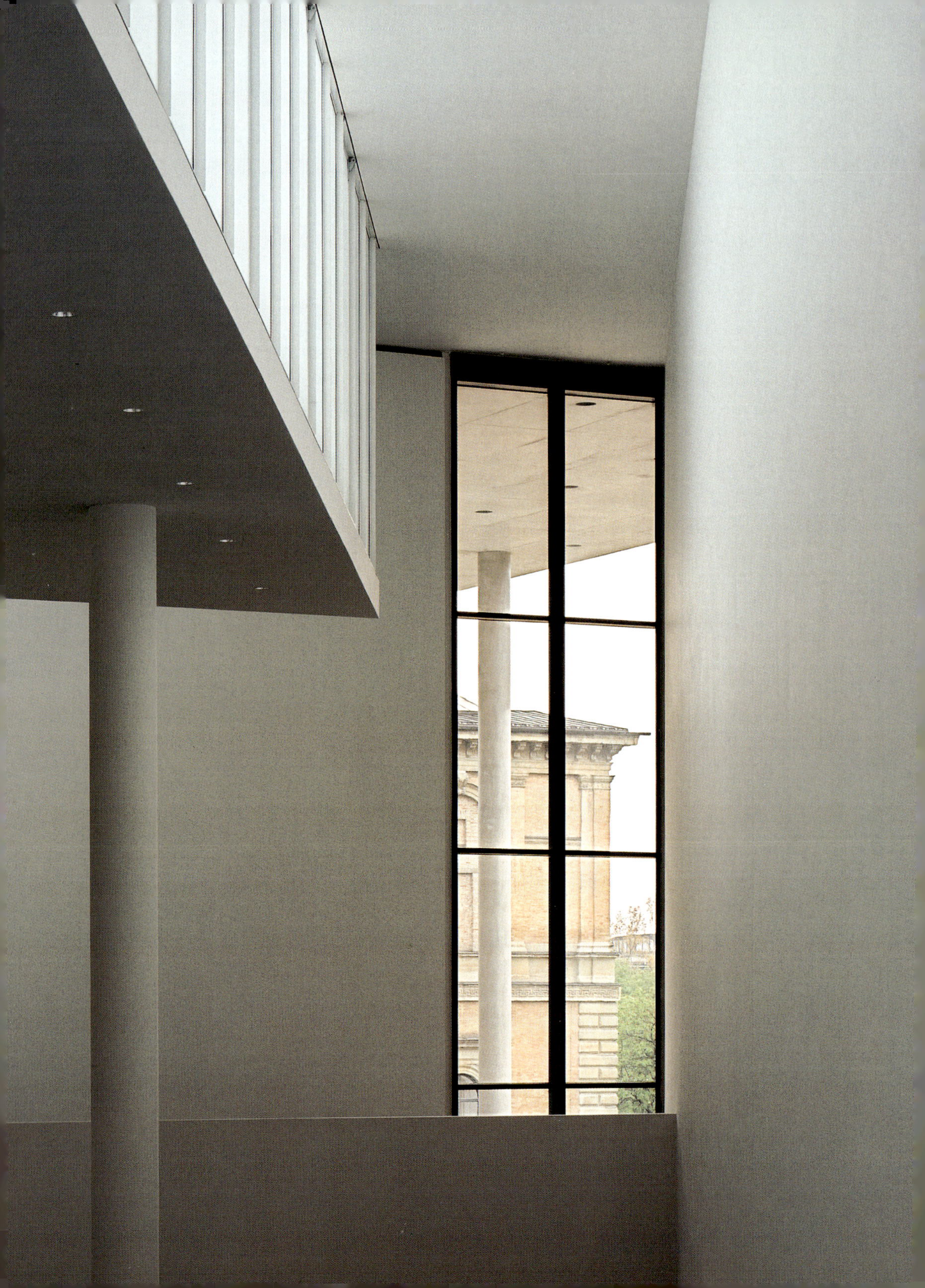

Gottfried Knapp

Stephan Braunfels Pinakothek der Moderne
München Munich

Architekturfotografie Architecture Photographs

Ulrich Schwarz

Prestel

München · Berlin · London · New York

Bayerische Staatsgemäldesammlungen, Staatsgalerie moderner Kunst: S. p. 45: Schenkung Sofie und Emanuel Fohn, S. p. 47 o. t.: Leihgabe Theo-Wormland-Stiftung, S. p. 47 u. b.: erw. m. Unterstützung der Theo-Wormland-Stiftung, S. p. 48 o. t., S. p. 49 u. b.: Leihgaben Verein Freunde zeitgenössischer Kunst für die Pinakothek der Moderne e.V., S. p. 48 u. b.: Vermächtnis Klaus Gebhard

Abbildungsnachweis Photo credits: Wenn nicht anders angegeben, stammen die Abbildungsvorlagen aus dem Archiv des Prestel Verlags mit Ausnahme von Unless otherwise indicated, the photographic material was taken from Prestel Verlag's archives, except for the following cases: Staatsgalerie moderner Kunst: S. pp. 44, 45 u. b. (ARTOTHEK; Fotos Photos: Joachim Blauel), S. p. 51 o. t.; Die Neue Sammlung: S. p. 56 (Foto Photo: D. Komma, München), S. pp. 57, 58 o. t. (Fotos Photos: Angela Bröhan, München), S. p. 58 u. b., S. p. 59 u. b. (Foto Photo: Klaus Frahm, Hamburg); Architekturmuseum: S. pp. 62, 63

Foto Photo S. p. 25: Jens Weber

Auf dem Umschlag On the cover (Vorderseite front; Rückseite back): Haupteingang Main entrance
Abbildungen Illustrations S. pp. 1, 3, 4: Rotunde, zweischalige Kuppel Rotunda, two-leaf cupola, Blick auf die Alte Pinakothek View of the Alte Pinakothek, Blick in die Rotunde View of the rotunda

Die Deutsche Bibliothek – CIP Einheitsaufnahme
Ein Titelsatz für diese Publikation ist bei der Deutschen Bibliothek erhältlich
The Library of Congress Cataloguing-in-Publication data is available

Prestel Verlag · Königinstraße 9 · 80539 München
Tel. +49 (089) 381709-0 · Fax +49 (089) 381709-35
www.prestel.de

4 Bloomsbury Place · London WC1A 2QA
Tel. +44 (020) 7323-5004 · Fax +44 (020) 7636-8004

175 5th Ave., Suite 402 · New York, NY 10010
Tel. +1 (212) 995-2720 · +1 (212) 995-2733
www.prestel.com

Prestel books are available worldwide. Please contact your nearest bookseller or write to one of the above addresses for information concerning your local distributor.

Texte zu den Sammlungen Texts on the collections:
Monika Wiedenmann

Translated from the German by Ishbel Flett

Projektmanagement Editorial direction:
Katharina Haderer-Wurm, Monika Wiedenmann
Lektorat Editor: Monika Wiedenmann
Gestaltung Design: WIGEL, München
Reproduktion Lithography: ReproLine, München
Druck und Bindung Printing and binding: sellier, Freising

Gedruckt auf chlorfrei gebleichtem Papier
Printed in Germany on acid-free paper

ISBN 3-7913-2831-X

Gottfried Knapp **Pinakothek der Moderne**

Die Pinakothek der Moderne ist nach der Alten Pinakothek und der Neuen Pinakothek das dritte große Haus der Bayerischen Kunstsammlungen in München. Sie fungiert als Museum für die Künste des 20. Jahrhunderts, nach dem Vorbild des berühmten Museum of Modern Art in New York, und bietet vier autonomen staatlichen Instituten, die bislang an verschiedenen Orten zu recht ungleichen Bedingungen agiert haben, ein großzügig dimensioniertes gemeinsames Präsentationsforum. Die Staatsgalerie moderner Kunst, die zuvor im Haus der Kunst weit unter Wert gehandelt worden war, die Neue Sammlung, eine der reichsten Design-Kollektionen der Welt, die in einem seitlichen Wurmfortsatz des Bayerischen Nationalmuseums immer nur Bruchteile ihrer Bestände hatte zeigen können, sowie die Graphische Sammlung und die Architektursammlung der Technischen Universität, die bislang gar keine eigenen Räume hatten, mit ihren hochrangigen Ausstellungen also auf die Gnade anderer Museen angewiesen waren, treten im neuen Gehäuse mit ihren Sammlungen und Sonderveranstaltungen erstmals gemeinsam an.

Doch die räumlichen Bedürfnisse der vier Sammlungsinstitute sind extrem unterschiedlich: Werke der Malerei – sie bilden den Kernbestand der Staatsgalerie – können sich in Oberlicht-Sälen am besten entfalten, Videoarbeiten und Installationen dagegen brauchen hermetisch abgedunkelte Räume; lichtempfindliche graphische Arbeiten, Zeichnungen und Fotografien sind in Kabinetten mit Seiten- oder Kunstlicht am besten

The Pinakothek der Moderne is the third in a group of major galleries housing the Bavarian Art Collections in Munich. As a museum dedicated to the art of the twentieth century, it is modelled along the lines of the famous Museum of Modern Art in New York and provides a broad platform for presenting the holdings of four separate state institutions previously scattered around the city. The institutions in question are the Staatsgalerie moderner Kunst, hitherto hidden away in the Haus der Kunst; the Neue Sammlung, one of the world's finest design collections, previously occupying an annexe of the Bayerisches Nationalmuseum, where only a tiny proportion of its works could be shown at any one time; and two collections of the Technische Universität—Prints & Drawings and Architecture—which had no premises of their own and were therefore entirely dependent on the cooperation of other museums as exhibition venues. Now these collections are being presented together for the very first time in a new home.

Each of these four collections demands its own specific environment. The paintings that form the core of the Staatsgalerie collection are best seen with natural overhead lighting, whereas the video works and installations need hermetically darkened rooms. Light-sensitive prints and drawings are best kept in cabinets lit from the side or by artificial lighting, whereas the design objects from the Neue Sammlung are so varied in size and shape that they require an equally heterogeneous variety of spaces.

aufgehoben; den extremen Größenunterschieden der Design-Objekte aus der Neuen Sammlung aber können nur Räume möglichst unterschiedlicher Dimension und Gestalt gerecht werden.

Der Architekt Stephan Braunfels hat die individuellen Raumwünsche der vier Museen im Rahmen seines strengen Grundrissrasters auf verblüffende Weise erfüllt. In seinem Haus gibt es Säle von einer halben bis zur dreifachen Stockwerkshöhe; Wände von extremer Länge und Höhe, die allen nur denkbaren Bildformaten gewachsen sind; quadratische, rechteckige und kreisrunde Einheiten, intime Kabinette, geräumige Säle und stützenfreie Hallen, in denen ganze Sonderausstellun-

Architect Stephan Braunfels has accommodated the individual needs of these four collections, exercising remarkable versatility within the framework of a stringently organised floor plan. The building features rooms with ceiling heights that vary from half a level to three full storeys. Walls of extreme length or height make it possible to display an enormous range of picture formats. There are square, rectangular and circular units, intimate cabinets, spacious rooms and vast halls free of pillars or supports, where an entire temporary exhibition can be mounted.

The focus of the composition is an enormous rotunda with cupola, reminiscent of the central pillared

Modellansicht Model view

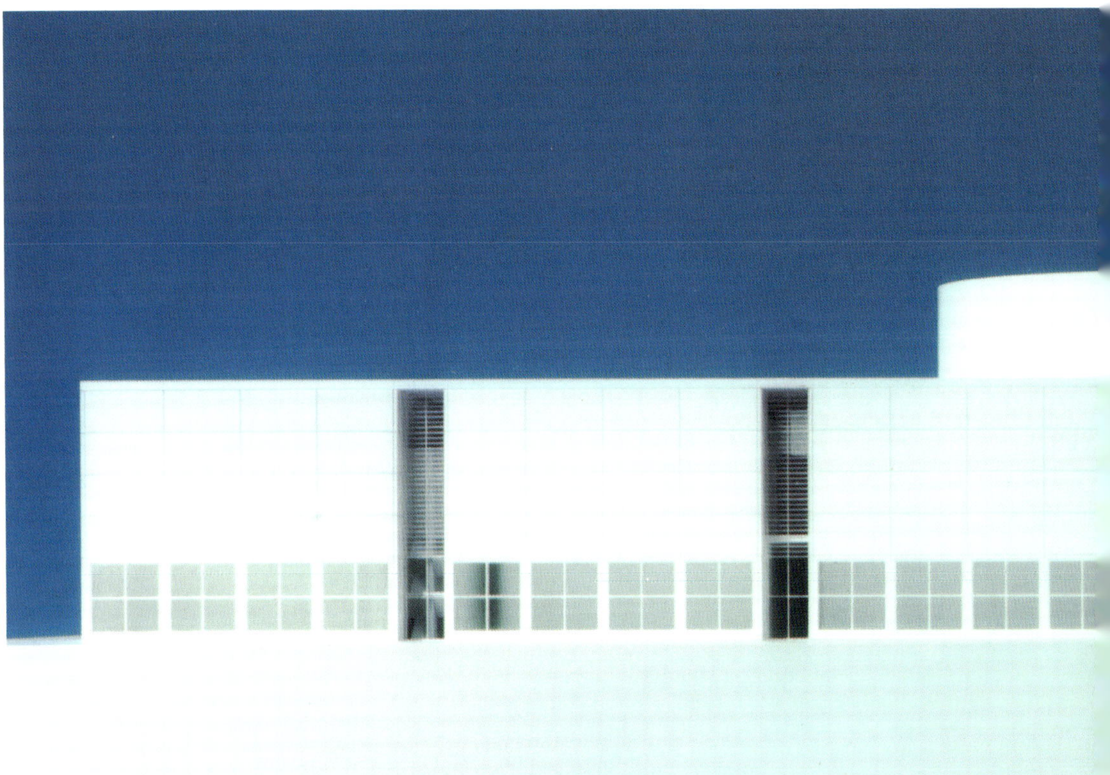

gen Platz finden. All diese Formen sind aus einer einzigen Großform entwickelt, die das Richtmaß für alle Grundrissformen und Unterteilungen im Haus ist.

Mittelpunkt der Komposition ist eine gewaltige Kuppelrotunde, die formal an die zentrale Säulenhalle im Alten Museum von Schinkel in Berlin erinnern will, aber sich nicht in repräsentativ-kultischen Aufgaben erschöpft, sondern als Eingangs- und Empfangshalle und als zentraler Verteiler eine wichtige funktionale Rolle im Gesamtkomplex übernimmt. Alle Museumsabteilungen und Servicebereiche in den drei öffentlichen Stockwerken des Hauses sind von der Rotunde aus direkt zugänglich.

hall of Schinkel's Altes Museum in Berlin, which does not merely pander to the wish for prestigious representation, but which actually plays an important functional role within the complex as a whole, forming an entrance and reception hall and central access area. All the museum departments and service facilities on the three levels of the building open to the public can be reached directly from the rotunda.

The central circular area is surrounded by the square that is reiterated on either side of the rectangular building and whose subdivisions provide the basic measure for the square alignment of the exhibition spaces as well as for the grid formation of square

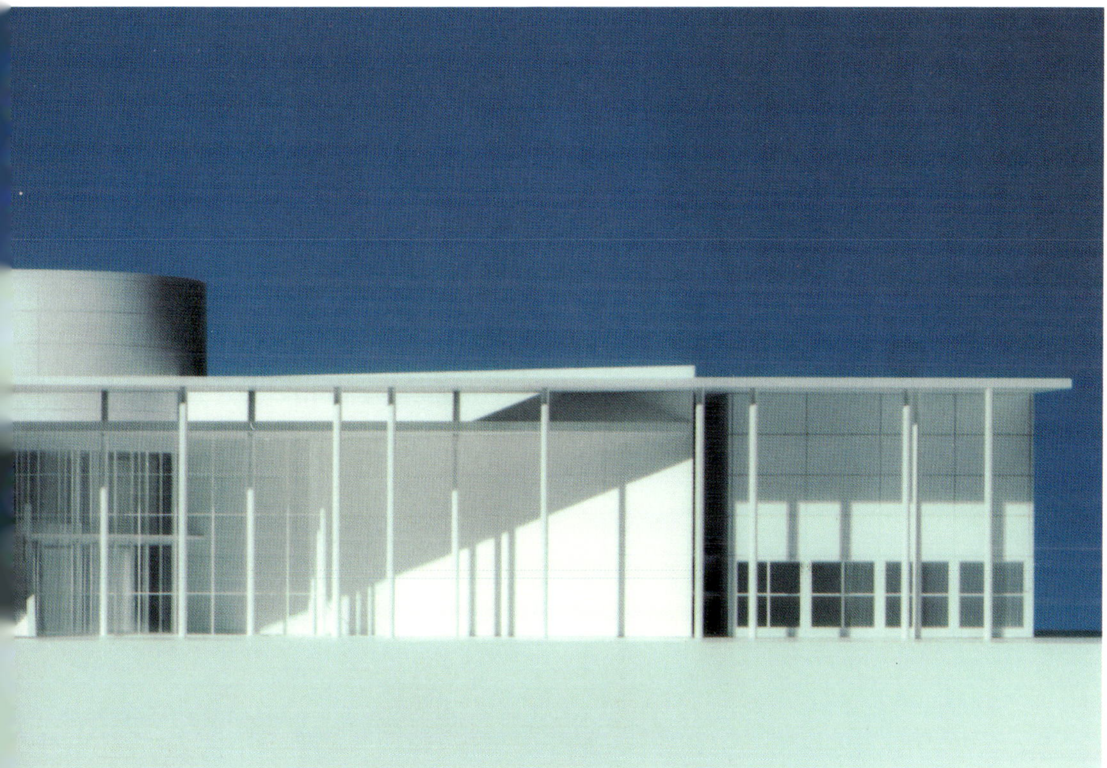

Lageplan Site plan

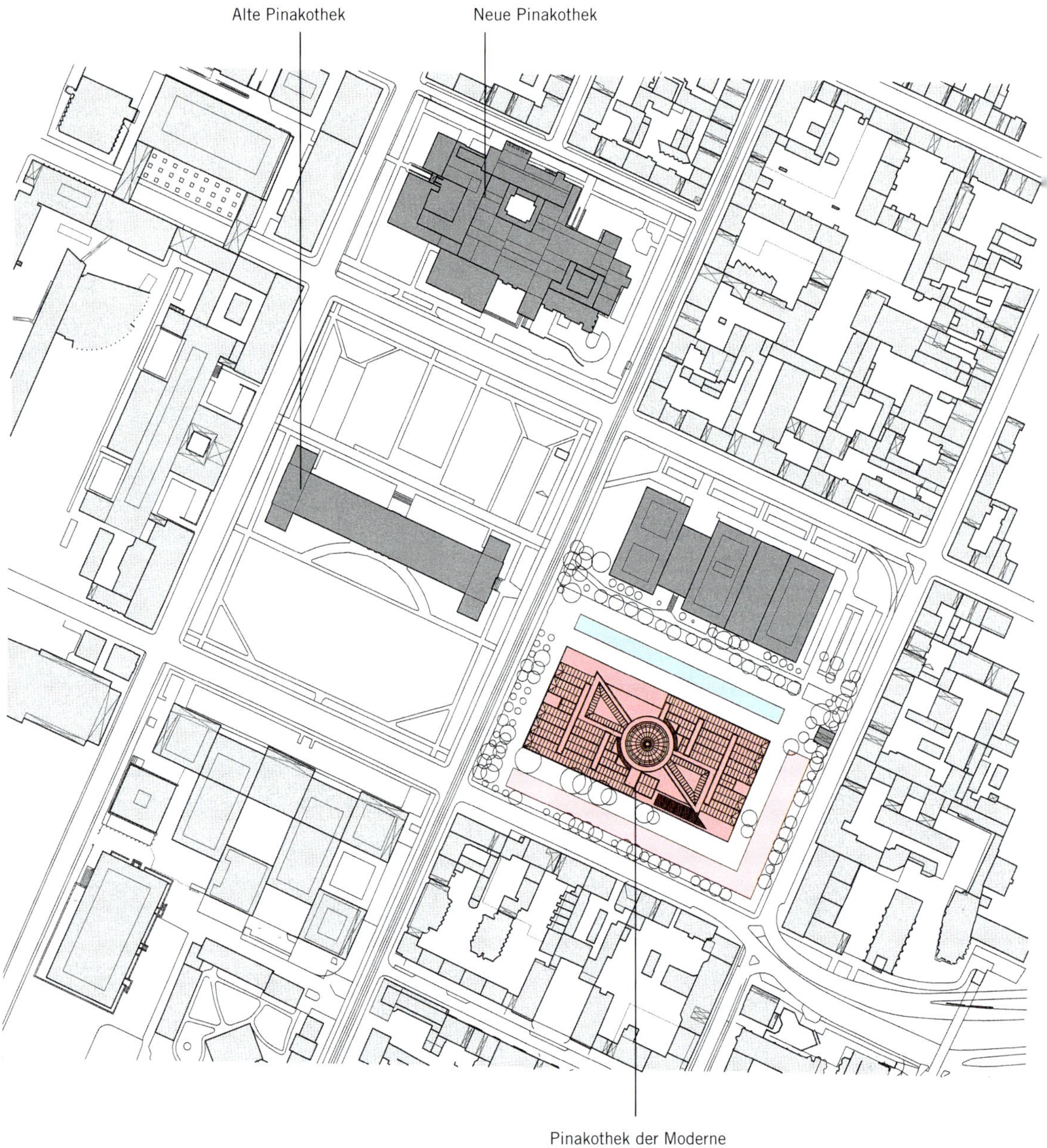

Der zentrale Grundrisskreis wird von jenem Quadrat umfangen, das in der Rechteckfigur des Hauses zu beiden Seiten jeweils noch einmal wiederkehrt und mit seinen Unterteilungen das Maß ist für die quadratische Ordnung der Ausstellungsräume, aber auch für den Raster der quadratischen Oberlichtkassetten, der dem gesamten Obergeschoss seinen fast magisch ruhigen Einheitsrhythmus gibt.

Diese orthogonale Ordnung wird durch eine kräftig wirksame Diagonale, eine schräg das Gebäude durchquerende Wand, die auf den Längsseiten im Norden wie im Süden beträchtliche Teile aus dem sonst geschlossenen Gebäudekubus herausschneidet, durchbrochen. Grund für diese doppelte öffnende Figur ist die städtebauliche Situation: Braunfels hat beim Architekten-Wettbewerb für das Museum als Einziger das Museum nach zwei Seiten – in Richtung Innenstadt und zu den anderen Pinakotheken hin – geöffnet. Die Besucher können also aus entgegengesetzten Richtungen in das Mittelrund gelangen, sie müssen von den öffentlichen Verkehrsmitteln aus keine Umwege auf sich nehmen, wenn sie das Museum, seinen Vortragssaal oder das ganztägig auch zur Straße hin geöffnete Café mit seinem riesigen Wintergarten und seinen geräumigen Freiflächen besuchen wollen.

Auf der Nordseite empfängt die Besucher, die von den anderen Pinakotheken herüberkommen und der einladenden Geste der herausfahrenden Diagonalwand folgen, eine offene hohe Pfeilerhalle. Sie bewährt sich als eine Art überdachtes Podium für Großskulpturen. Durch das mächtige gläserne Vestibül geht es hinein in die hohe, weite Rotunde, die über das Koordinatenkreuz der erschließenden Flure und über die diagonale Blickachse fast alle Funktionen ins Bild rückt, also die Ordnung des Gebäudes fast beiläufig erschließt.

Im Ostteil des Erdgeschosses, wo auch die Büroräume und die Fachbibliothek der Neuen Sammlung liegen, sind die fünf großen, beliebig kombinier- und unterteilbaren Wechselausstellungsräume der Graphischen Sammlung und der Architektursammlung nach Norden hin orientiert. Hohe Atelierfenster und eine zurückgenommene Lichtdecke sorgen dort für eine schonende, teils natürliche, teils technisch kontrollierte Helligkeit.

skylight cassettes that lends the entire upper floor its almost magical air of calm serenity and rhythmic unity.

This orthogonal order is interrupted by the striking force of a diagonal wall that shears right through the building, slicing huge swathes out of an otherwise closed cube. The reason for the openness and duality of this space is the urban situation: Braunfels was the only architect to submit a design that envisaged having the museum open up on two sides—towards the city centre and towards the other Pinakothek buildings. In this way, people arriving by public transport can enter the central rotunda from different directions without any detours when visiting the museum, its auditorium or the street-facing café that is open all day, with its spacious wintergarden and open-air zones.

On the north side, visitors arriving from the other Pinakothek buildings follow the welcoming gesture of the protruding diagonal wall to enter the open and high-ceilinged pillared hall, which is ideally suited as a kind of covered podium for large-scale sculptures. The huge glazed vestibule leads into the sweeping space of the high rotunda, where the diagonal axis brings almost all the functions of the building into view, lending the order and overall structure of the complex an impression of seemingly effortless transparency.

In the eastern part of the ground floor, where the offices and the specialist library of the Neue Sammlung are located, we find the five large north-facing exhibition spaces that can be partitioned as required for temporary exhibitions of the Prints & Drawings Collection and the Architectural Collection. High studio windows and a recessed skylit ceiling provide subtle lighting that is part natural and part technically controlled.

The diagonal walls, which, on the exterior, create the wedge-shaped entrance halls, also form huge trapezoidal spaces opening out from the rotunda. Braunfels has modelled the main stairs of the building with an astonishing sense of perspective: on the one hand, they sweep grandly down into the sequence of ground floor rooms housing the Neue Sammlung, while, on the other hand, they lead visitors up through a bright, large and ever widening space into the skylit galleries of the Staatsgalerie, designed to take even the largest canvases.

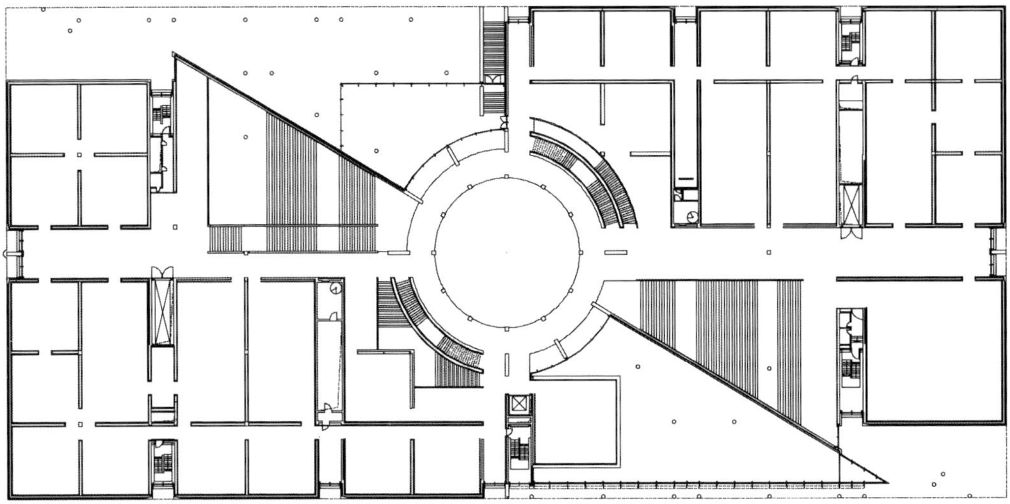

Grundriss 1. Obergeschoss Upper floor plan

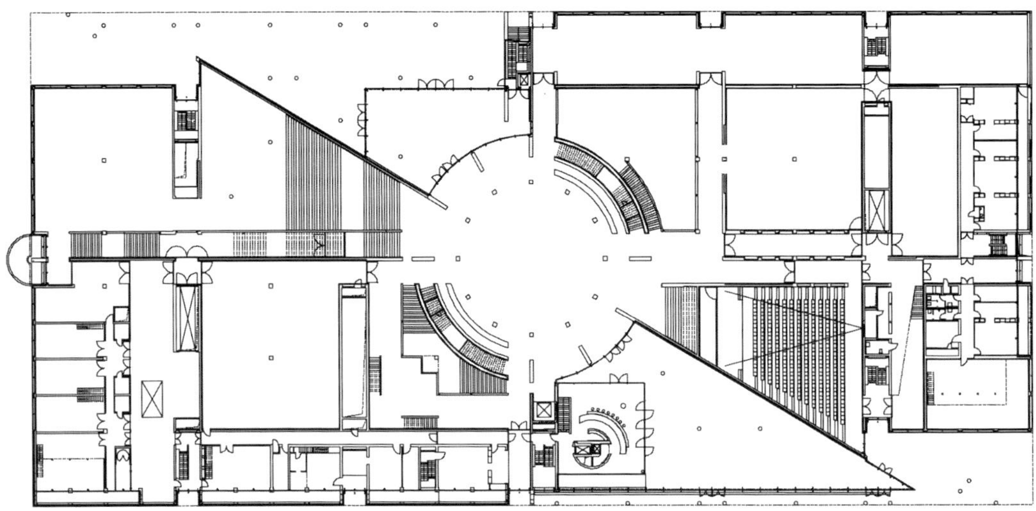

Grundriss Erdgeschoss Ground floor plan

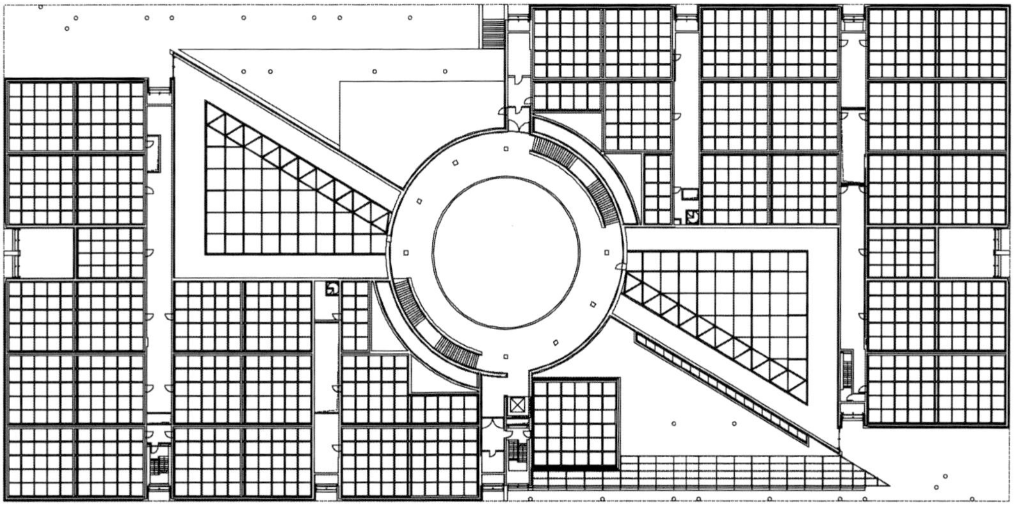

Grundriss Galeriegeschoss Gallery floor plan

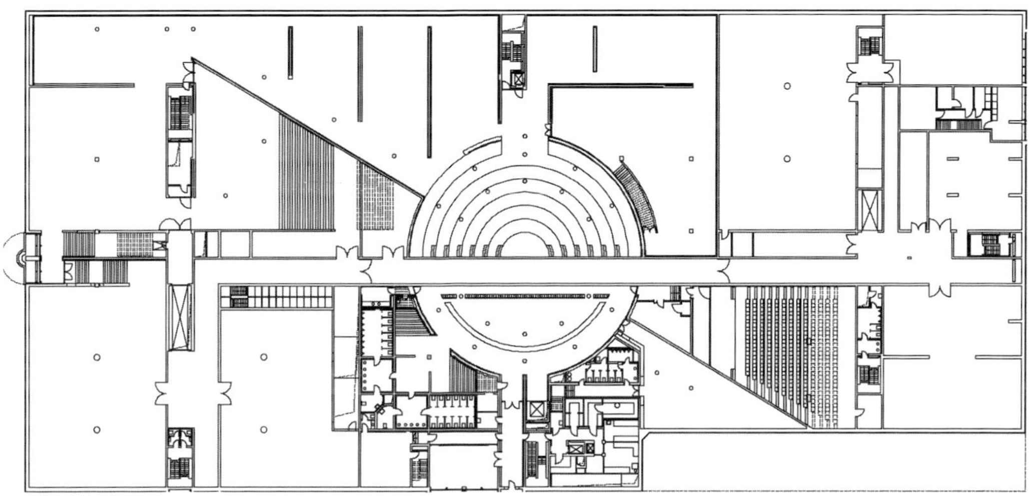

Grundriss 1. Untergeschoss Lower floor plan

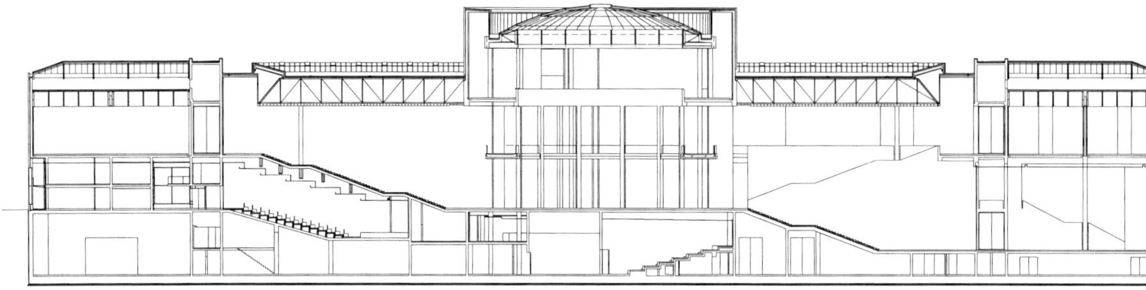

Längsschnitt Longitudinal section

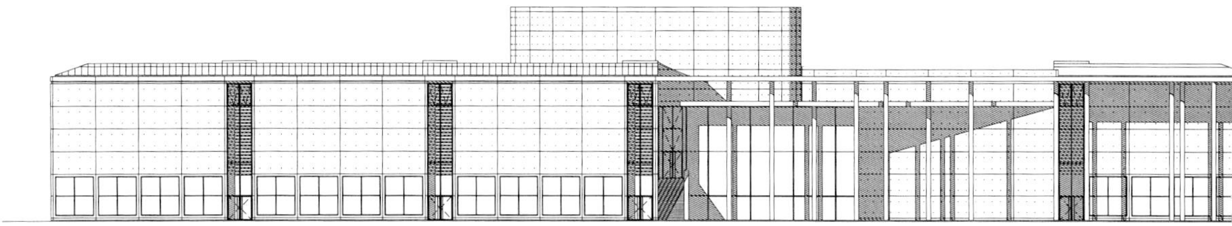

Ansicht Nord North view

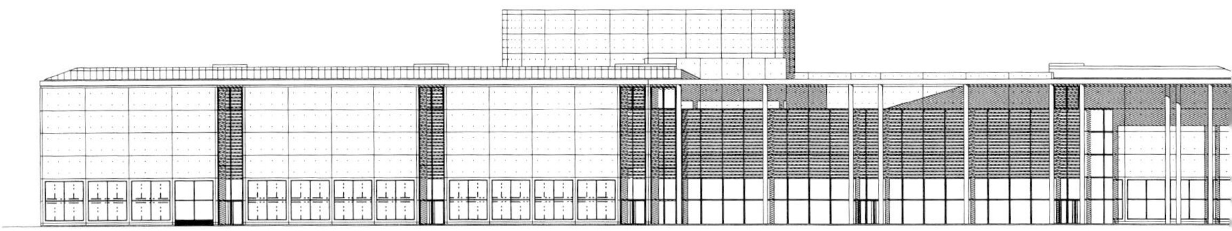

Ansicht Süd South view

Ansicht West / Ost West / east view

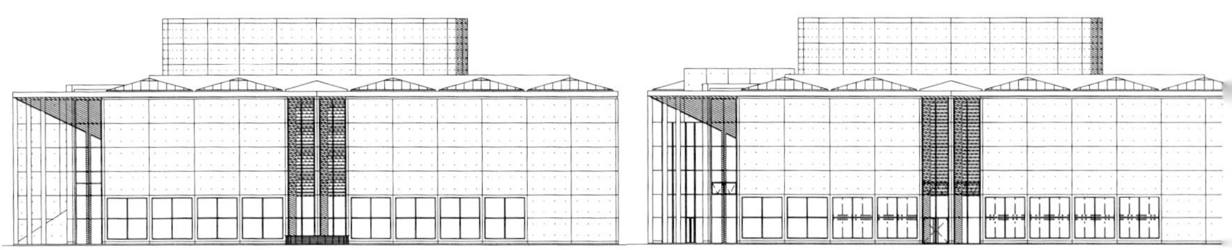

Die Diagonalwände, die mit ihrer Außenseite den Eingangshallen ihre Keilform geben, formen im Inneren trapezartig von der Rotunde aus sich öffnende riesige Räume. In ihre perspektivisch verblüffende Weite hat Braunfels die Haupttreppen des Hauses hineinmodelliert; auf der einen Seite geht es in grandioser Geste hinab in die Raumfolge der Neuen Sammlung im Untergeschoss, auf der anderen steigen die Besucher in einer sich weitenden hellen Halle, die auf größte Bildformate abgestimmt ist, hinauf in die Oberlichtsäle der Staatsgalerie.

Beim Weg hinab kann man die breite Treppenschräge fast als ein Stück Arena empfinden; jedenfalls lädt der über drei Stockwerke sich erstreckende Raum mit seiner begleitenden Aufwärtstreppe und der Empore zu Konzerten, Modeschauen oder Design-Präsentationen geradezu ein. Im doppelgeschossigen, stützenfreien ersten Hauptraum der Sammlung – er kann auch von außen eingesehen werden – lassen sich ganze Autoschauen veranstalten. Dennoch ist es ein großer Gewinn, dass der gleich danebenliegende, noch um ein Geschoss tiefer in die Erde hinunterreichende große Depotraum der Sammlung – er eignet sich vorzüglich für Inszenierungen mit Werkstattcharakter – den Ausstellungshallen als doppelgeschossig begehbares Magazin zugeschlagen wurde.

Darüber, im Erdgeschoss, sind die Räume für Wechselausstellungen untergebracht. Der große Kunstlichtraum im Westtrakt ist für Videoinstallationen reserviert; die nach Norden geöffneten Seitenlichtsäle und die anschließenden Räume im Osttrakt werden von der Architektursammlung und der Graphischen Sammlung je nach Bedarf bespielt.

Das gesamte Obergeschoss mit der schier endlosen Folge seiner Oberlichtsäle ist der Staatsgalerie moderner Kunst zugedacht. Wer dort den historischen Rundgang in zeitlich logischer Reihenfolge absolvieren will, der beginnt am besten bei den Expressionisten im Westen, wo die quadratischen Raumeinheiten sich teilweise kleeblattförmig zusammenschließen, also nur von einer Ecke aus erschlossen werden, was den Rundgang wesentlich erleichtert. In allen Oberlichtsälen verblüffen die fast schattenfreie Helligkeit und die konsequente Absenz jeglicher störender Installationen. Und wer den Verhau aus Hinweisschildern, Steckdosen

On the way down, the broad sweep of the stairs is reminiscent of the descent into an arena. The three-storey space with its steps and gallery certainly lends itself perfectly to staging such events as concerts, fashion shows or design presentations. In the two-storey, support-free first main room of the collection—visible from the outside—even major automobile shows can be presented. At the same time, the adjacent depot room, which goes one level deeper, is ideal for workshop-style presentations. The linkage of these two spaces is an enormous gain.

Above, on the ground floor, are the temporary exhibition spaces. The large artificially lit room in the western tract is reserved for video installations; the side-lit rooms that open towards the north and the adjacent rooms in the eastern tract are used for the Architectural Collection and the Prints & Drawings Collections, as required.

The entire upper floor with its seemingly endless sequence of skylit rooms has been earmarked for the Staatsgalerie moderner Kunst. Those who wish to view the works in chronological order are advised to begin with the Expressionists in the western tract, where the square units are conveniently aligned in trefoil form. In all the skylit rooms, the most striking impression is one of almost shadowless brightness, devoid of all distracting installations. Anyone who has ever noticed the ramshackle jumble of signs, power points and ventilators with which many a famous architect has littered museum buildings is in for a pleasant surprise.

Daylight pours into the two-metre high glazed zone through the ceiling cassettes, where it is collected, mixed and filtered down without manipulation through glass panels into the exhibition spaces. The ventilation sources are concealed in the floors at the edges, and the air vents are concealed in the ceilings. No technical fittings break the smooth continuity of the walls and, since the doorways between the rooms are open all the way to the ceiling, while the grey terrazzo floors continue uninterruptedly through them, the view through a sequence of rooms opens up exciting perspectives, with brilliant nuances of subtly differing whites on the ceilings and walls.

Braunfels, however, achieves the most remarkable spatial handling of all with his two-leaf cylinder inserted

und Belüftungseinrichtungen in Erinnerung hat, den manche berühmten Architekten in ihren Museumsbauten hinterlassen haben, der kann hier nur staunen.

Das Tageslicht, das in der zwei Meter hohen, glasgedeckten Zone über den Deckenkassetten gesammelt, gemischt, gefiltert und durch die dämpfenden Glasplatten hinunter in die Säle geschickt wird, enthält sich jeder manipulierenden Einflussnahme. Die Quelllüftungen sind in den Rändern am Boden, die Abzugsöffnungen in den Deckenkassetten versteckt. Auch die Wände bleiben in ganzer Höhe frei von störenden Elementen; und da die Portale zwischen den Räumen bis zur Kassettendecke hinauf geöffnet sind, die grauen Terrazzoböden aber durch die Tore hindurchlaufen, ergeben sich beim Blick durch mehrere hintereinandergelagerte Räume aufregende Perspektiven, die mit diversen Abstufungen von kühlem oder wärmerem Weiß an Decken und Wänden brillieren.

Die überraschendsten Raumkreationen gelingen Braunfels aber mit dem ins Zentrum des Rechteckkubus hineingesetzten doppelschaligen Zylinder. Dieses gewaltige Kuppelrund mit seinen zwölf tragenden Säulen, mit den achsialen Durchblicken bis hinaus ins Freie, mit der runden Außenwand und den fast dramatisch auf die Zylinderform reagierenden anliegenden Räumen gehört zweifellos zu den eindrucksvollsten Raumschöpfungen im internationalen Museumsbau der letzten Jahre. In der doppelschichtig gekurvten Wand führen Treppen aus dem Erdgeschoss nach oben ins Galeriegeschoss und weiter auf die kreisrunde Ausstellungs-Empore unter der Glaskuppel, die einen schönen Tiefblick in die unteren Geschosse eröffnet und mit ihrer vom Tageslicht suggestiv modellierten hohen weißen Umfassungswand einen gewaltigen Rundhorizont darstellt.

Um den mächtig herausragenden Zylinder im Zentrum des Baus läuft in der Höhe des Hauptdachs noch einmal ein gläserner Oberlichtring herum. Durch ihn fällt das Tageslicht hinter den Rundwänden bis hinunter ins Untergeschoss; es setzt die kubisch eindrucksvollen Formationen der angelagerten Teile, etwa den Würfel des Museumsladens, effektvoll ins Bild.

Auch alle übrigen Funktionen im Gebäude sind konsequent aus dem ›gebundenen System‹ entwickelt: aus dem zentralen Kreis, dem ihn umgebenden Qua-

into the centre of the cube. This massive cupola with its twelve load-bearing columns and axial views towards the exterior, the round outer wall and the almost dramatic response of the adjacent rooms to the cylindrical form is undoubtedly one of the most impressive spatial compositions to be found anywhere in the field of recent international museum architecture. In the curved two-leaf wall, stairs lead up from the ground floor to the gallery floor and on to the circular raised exhibition area beneath the glass cupola. From this vantage point, with its high white walls evocatively moulded by the natural light to appear like a vast horizon, there is a magnificent view down into the lower levels.

A skylight ring at the level of the main roof encircles the enormous cylinder at the centre of the building, allowing natural light to fall all the way to the basement level behind the round walls. This effectively highlights the impressive cubic formation of other elements such as the cube forming the museum shop.

All the other functions of the building have been consistently developed on the basis of the "composite system": the central circle, the surrounding square, the two squares of equal size on either side and the diagonal that cuts through the composition. For instance, Braunfels has fitted the basement level cloakrooms into a segment of the central rotunda; he has modelled a seven-step amphitheatre into the other semi-circle, which forms a superb platform for a display of chairs from the Neue Sammlung. In the hollow space of the circular crypt beneath, the jewellery collection of the Danner Foundation will be shown as in a treasury. Even the large auditorium that sinks from the ground floor to the basement level, slotting quite naturally in beneath the stairwell leading to the upper floor, is an exercise in wasting not a scrap of available space.

Both in terms of formal structure and as a functional museum facility, the Pinakothek der Moderne is a clear counterpoint to the bombastically gesticulating sculpturality of Frank O. Gehry's Guggenheim Museum in Bilbao. Anyone who has ever been to Bilbao has enthused about the remarkable architecture, but few bother to mention the works on display inside. The works of art themselves are little more than superfluous, changing decor for the main exhibit—Gehry's monu-

drat, den beiden seitlich angelagerten gleich großen Quadraten und der die Ordnung durchschneidenden Diagonale. So hat Braunfels etwa die Garderoben im Untergeschoss in ein Segment der zentralen Rotunde eingepasst; in das andere Halbrund hat er ein siebenstufiges Amphitheater modelliert, das mit seinen gekurvten Rängen der Stühle-Kollektion der Neuen Sammlung einen verblüffenden Auftritt verschafft. In dem Hohlraum darunter, einer Ringkrypta, soll einmal die Schmucksammlung der Danner-Stiftung wie in einer Schatzkammer zelebriert werden. Sogar der große Vortragssaal, der sich vom Erdgeschoss aus ins Untergeschoss absenkt, ist im Grunde einem Restraum abgewonnen. Unter der Treppenhalle, die hinaufführt ins Obergeschoss, ist die gestufte Anlage des Mehrzwecksaals fast natürlich eingepasst.

Nicht nur formal, sondern auch museumstechnisch ist die Pinakothek der Moderne also das entschiedene Gegenbild zu Frank O. Gehrys bombastisch gestikulierender Guggenheim-Skulptur in Bilbao. Wer je in Bilbao war, hat den mitreißenden Schwung dieser Schau-Architektur gerühmt, doch keiner hat je eines der ausgestellten Kunstwerke erwähnt; die Exponate sind dort nur überflüssiger, wechselnder Dekor für das eigentliche Ausstellungsstück, die computergenerierte Monumentalplastik Gehrys, die keine Formen neben oder unter sich duldet.

Braunfels hat in seinem Münchner Museumsbau alle Formen aus einem strengen Grundrissraster entwickelt und dabei in den Kommunikations- und Zubringerbereichen einige eindrucksvolle Räume und Durchblicke geschaffen. Dort aber, wo die Kunstwerke wirken sollen, in den Ausstellungssälen, hat er die Architektur mit subtilen Mitteln zum Schweigen gebracht. In München ist also ein Museum für die Kunst des 20. Jahrhunderts entstanden, das sich ausstellungstechnisch mit jedem anderen Museumsneubau der Welt messen kann, den Exponaten dabei zu bester Wirkung verhilft und doch nicht im funktionalen oder formalen Schematismus erstirbt.

mental computer-generated sculpture, which brooks no other forms alongside it.

In Braunfels' Munich museum building, all the forms are developed on the basis of a stringent floor plan, thereby creating thoroughly impressive areas of access and communications. However, in the actual exhibition spaces, where the works of art themselves are meant to be seen, the architecture has been subtly silenced. Munich now has a museum of twentieth-century art to rival any new museum building in the world. It provides an effective setting for the exhibits that does not merely dwindle into functional or formal schematism.

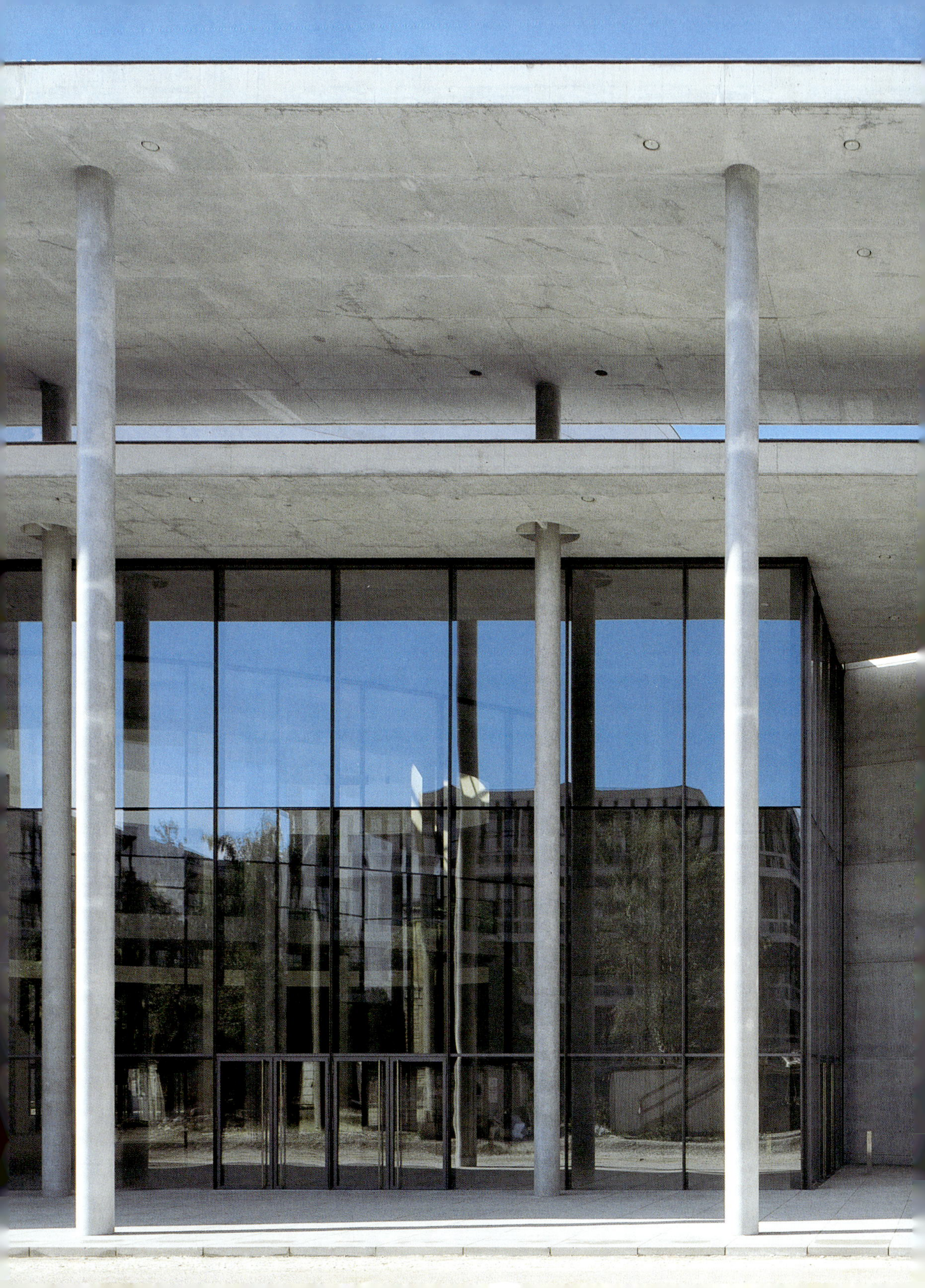

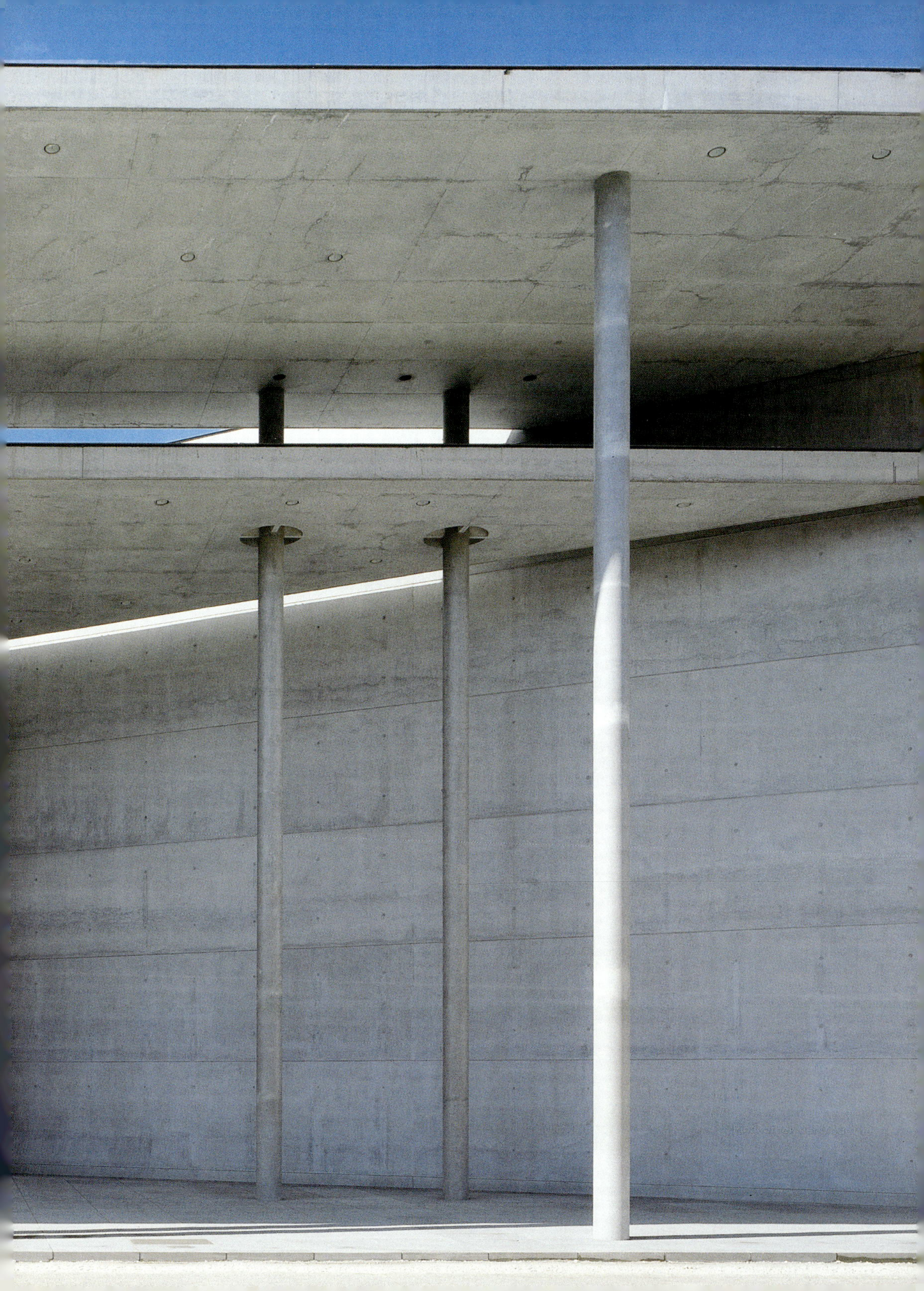

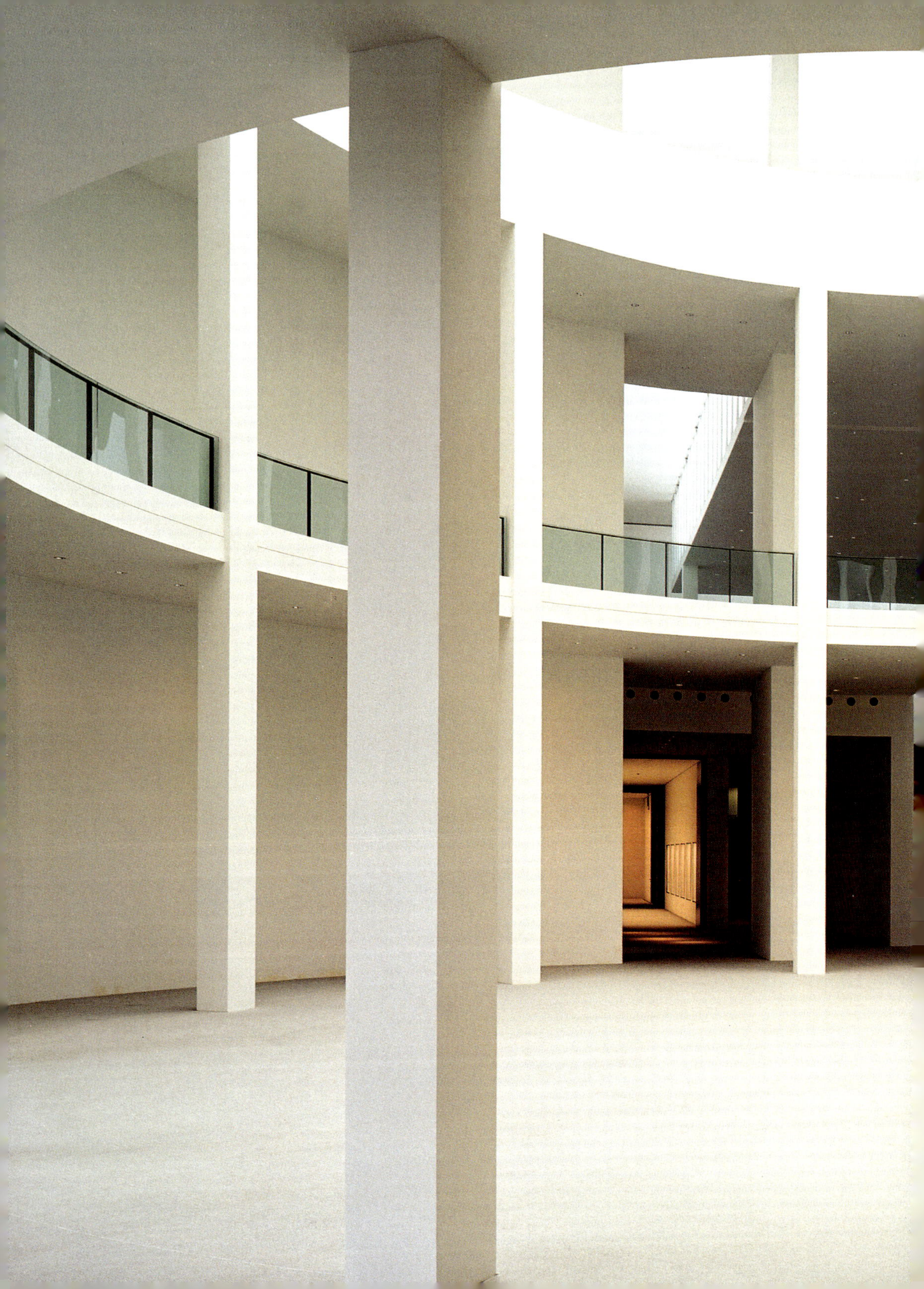

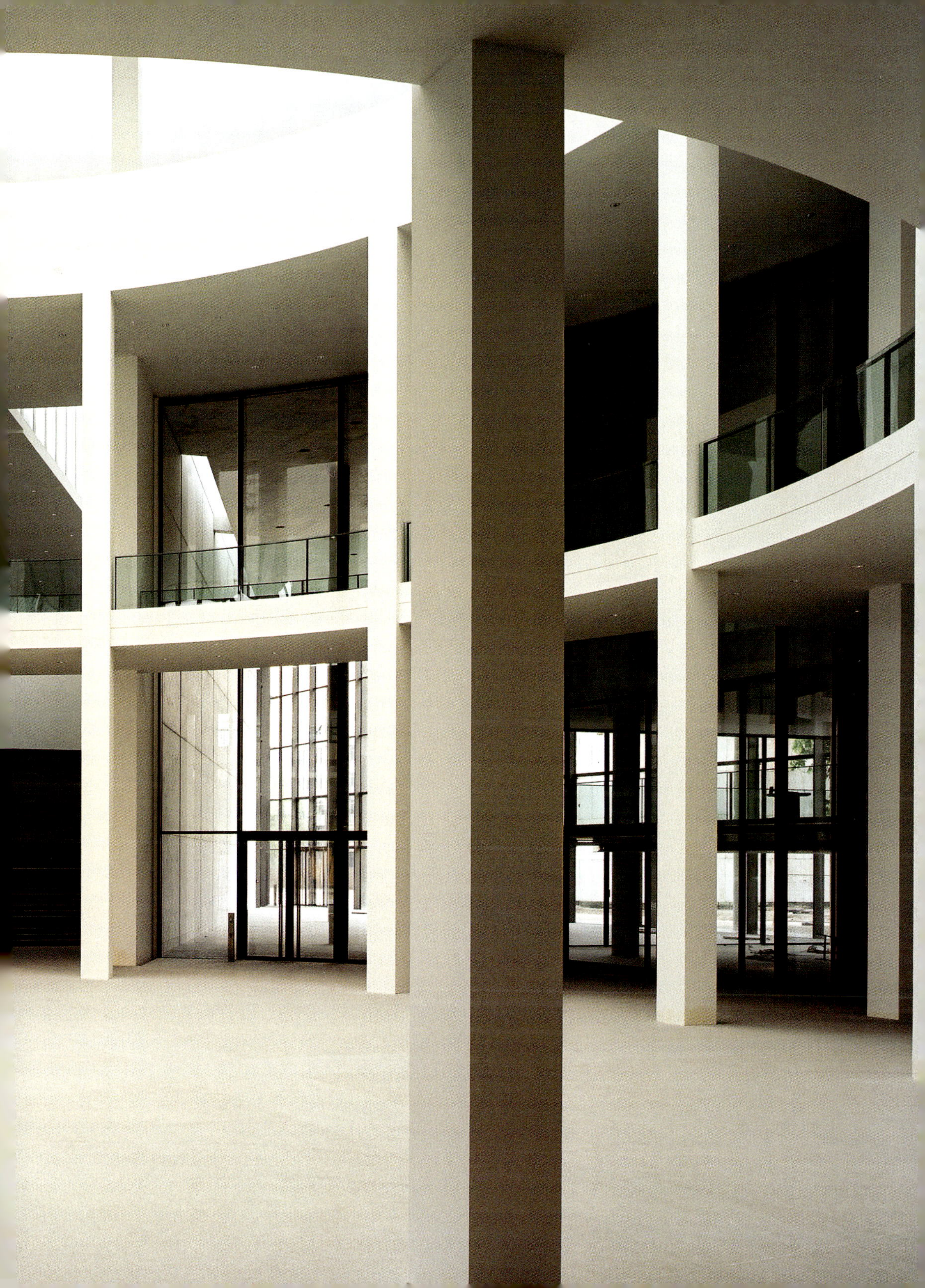

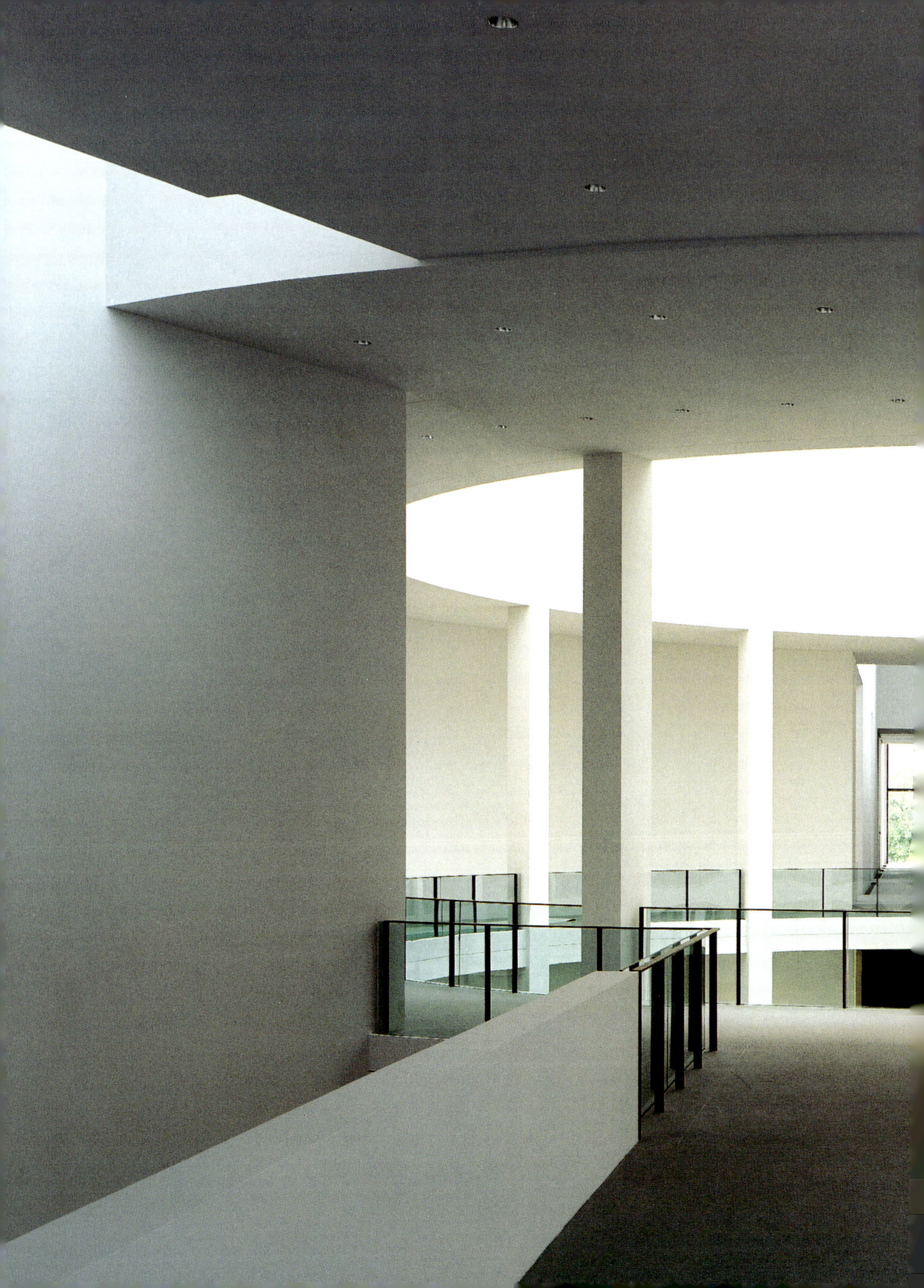

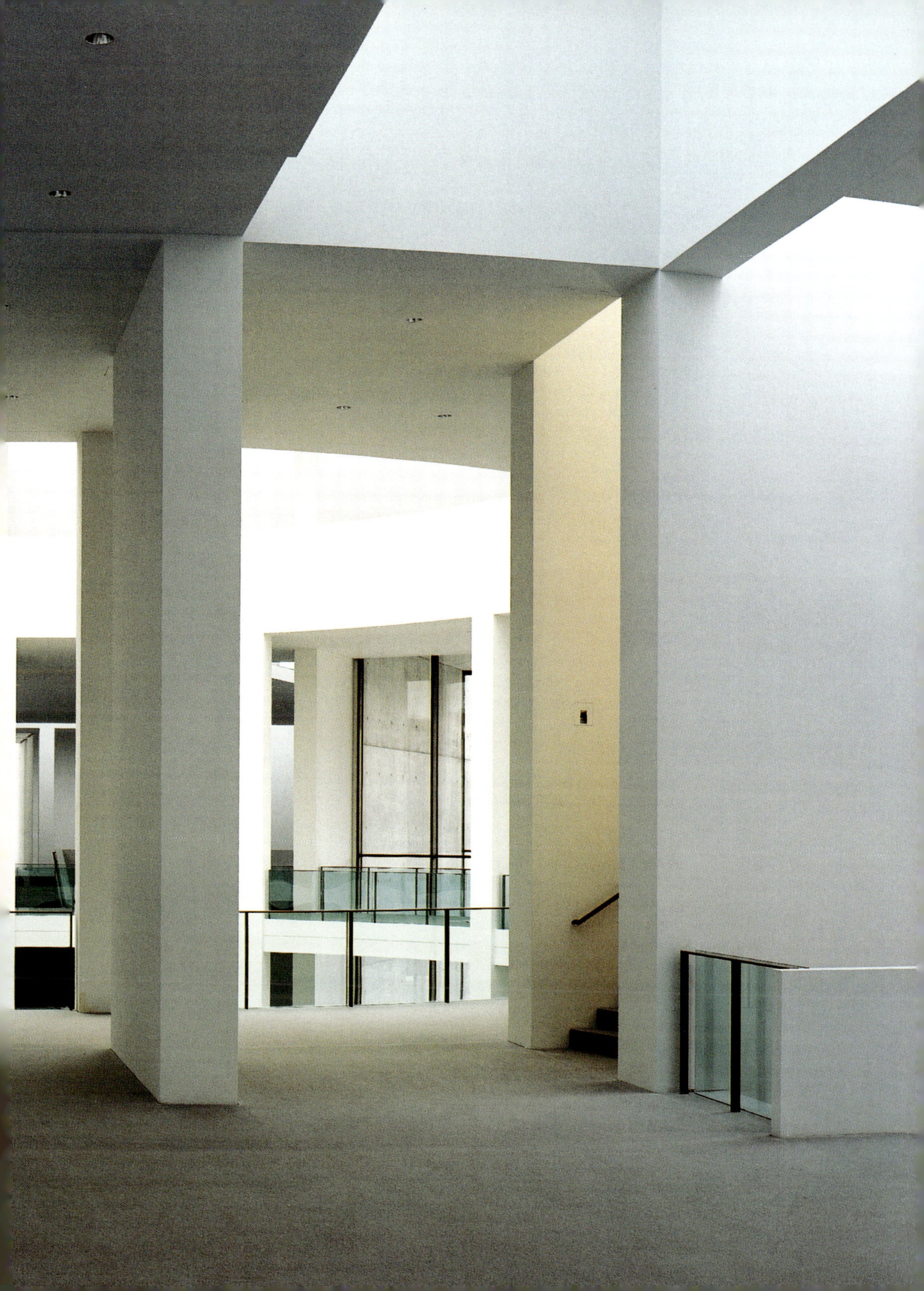

<<< Ansicht Nord, Haupteingang North view, main entrance

<< Rotunde mit Blick in den Wintergarten Rotunda and view into the wintergarden

< Blick in die Rotunde View of the rotunda

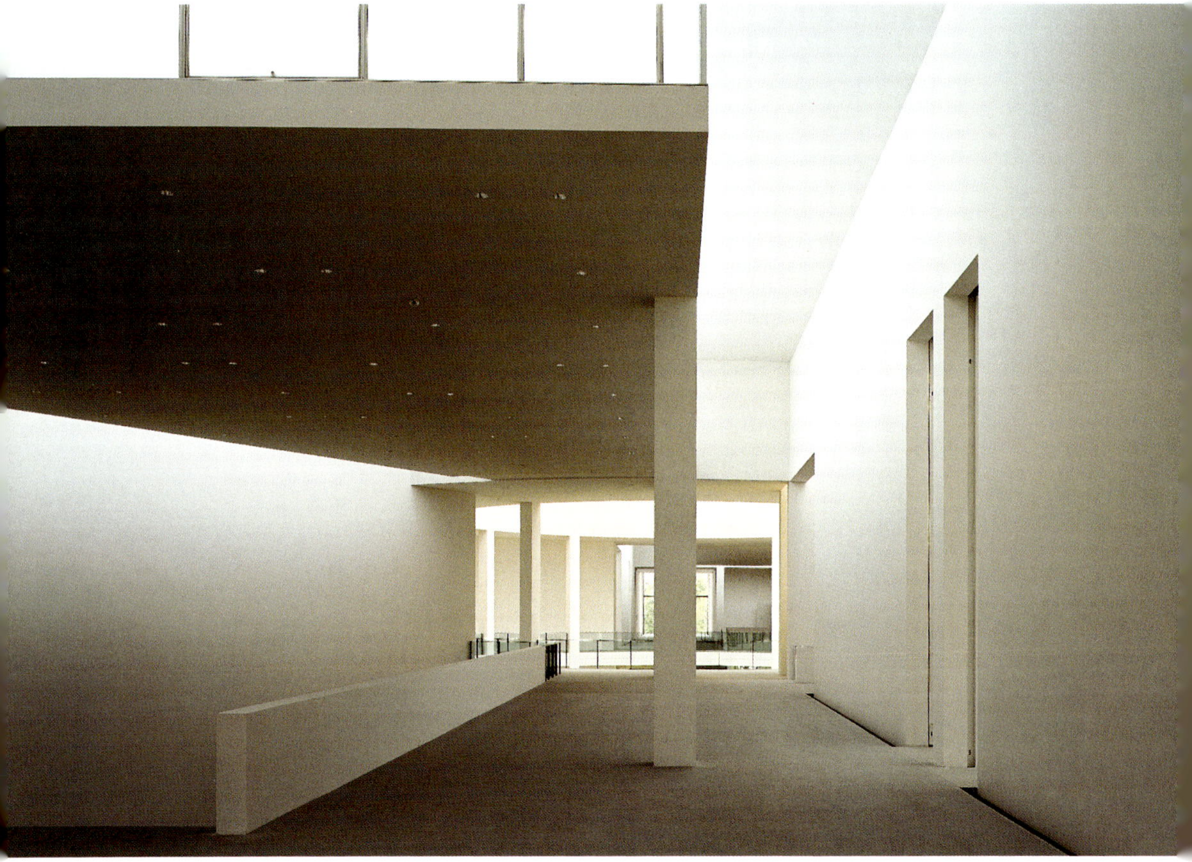

Ausstellungsflächen rings um die Rotunde Exhibition areas around the rotunda

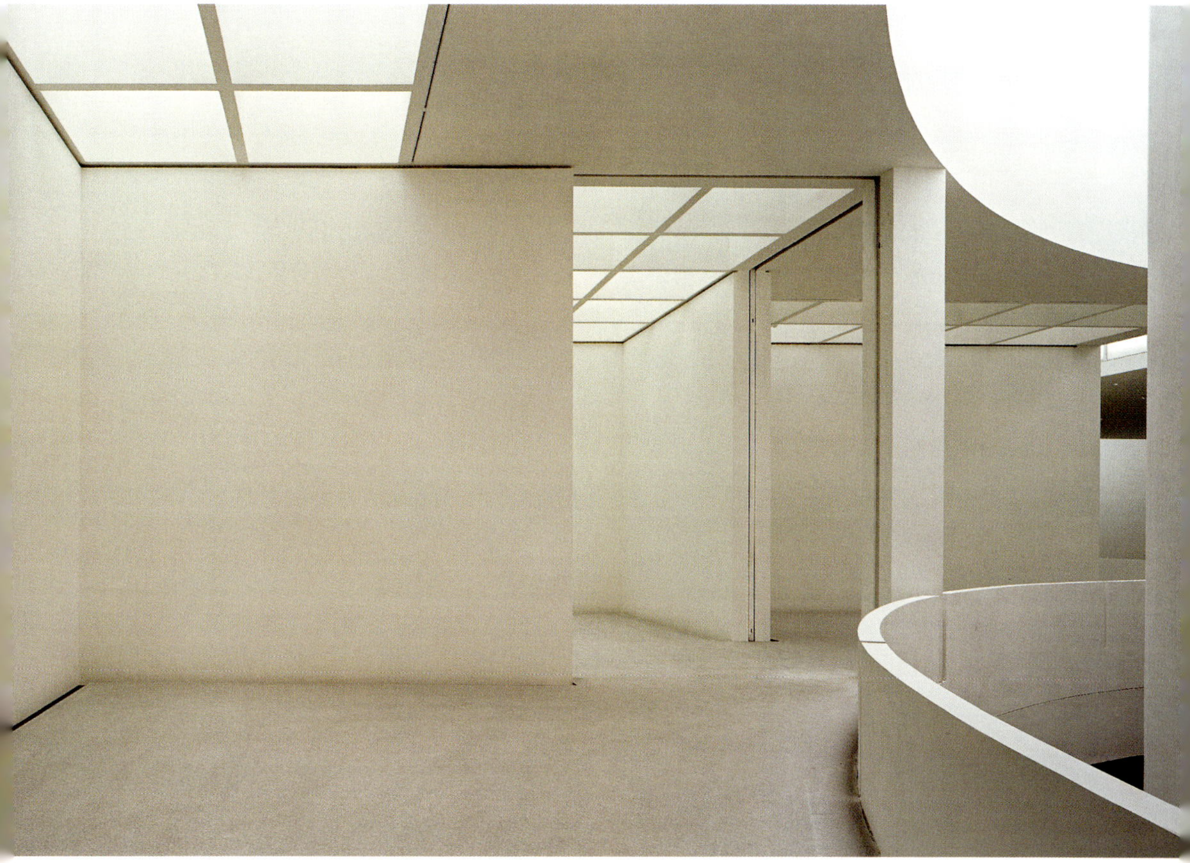

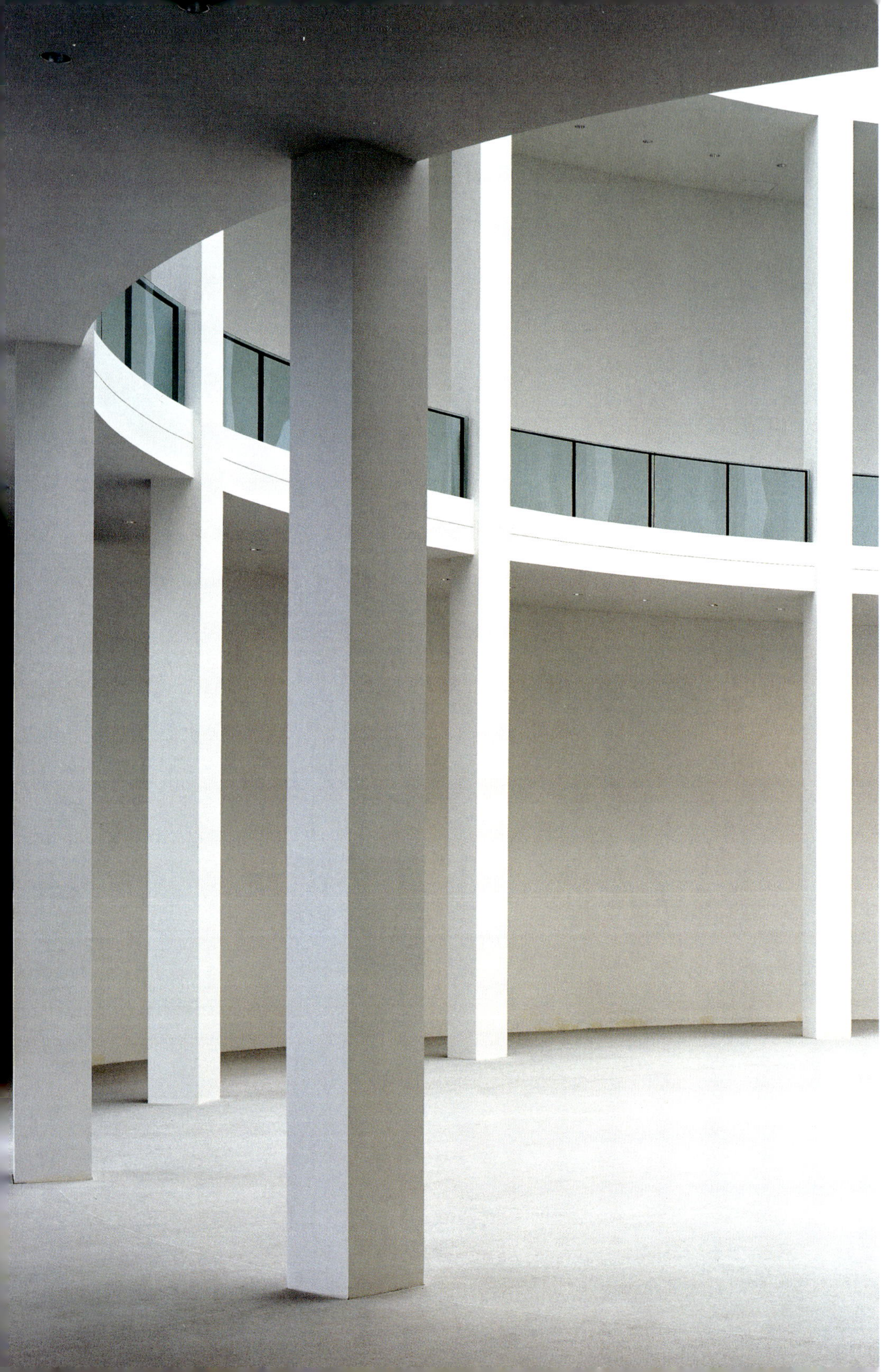

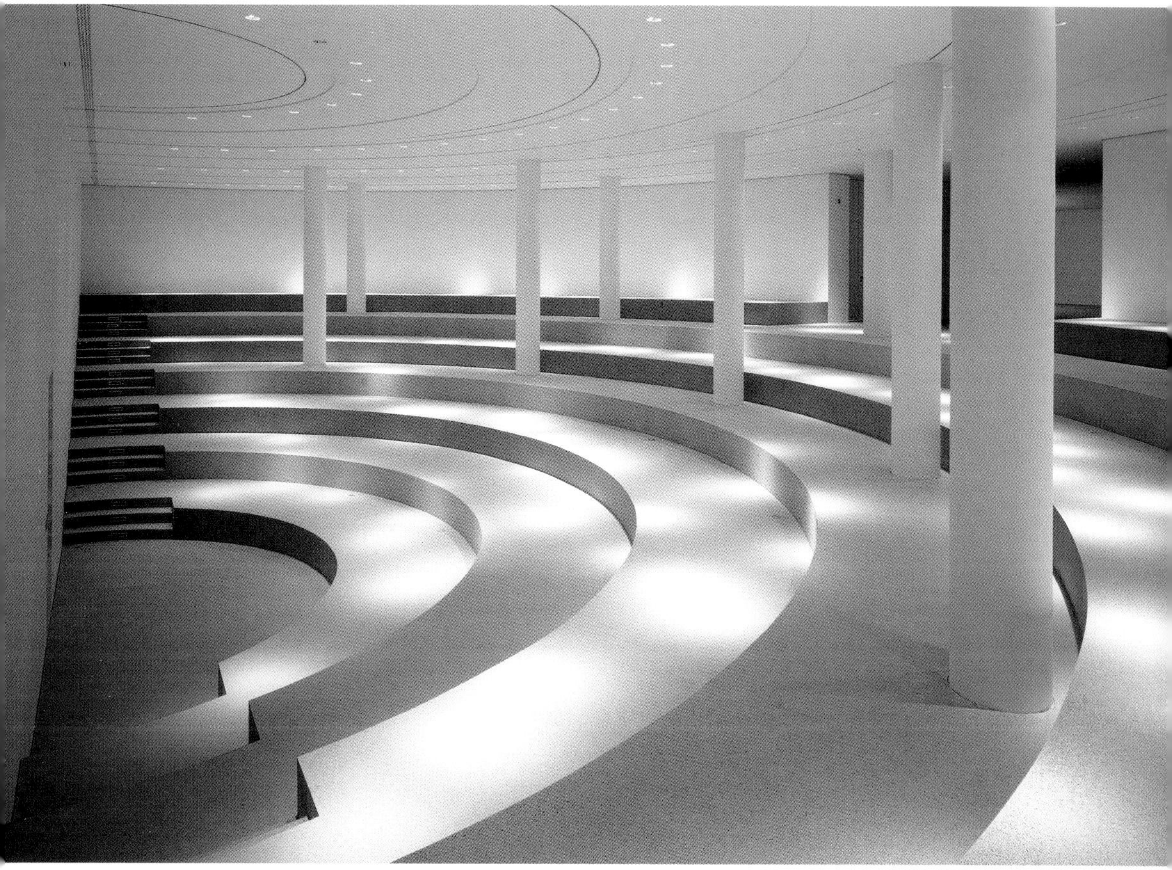

Rotunde mit Galerie Rotunda and gallery

Amphitheater für die Thonetsammlung Amphitheatre for the Thonet Collection

Rotunde, zweischalige Kuppel Rotunda, two-leaf cupola >

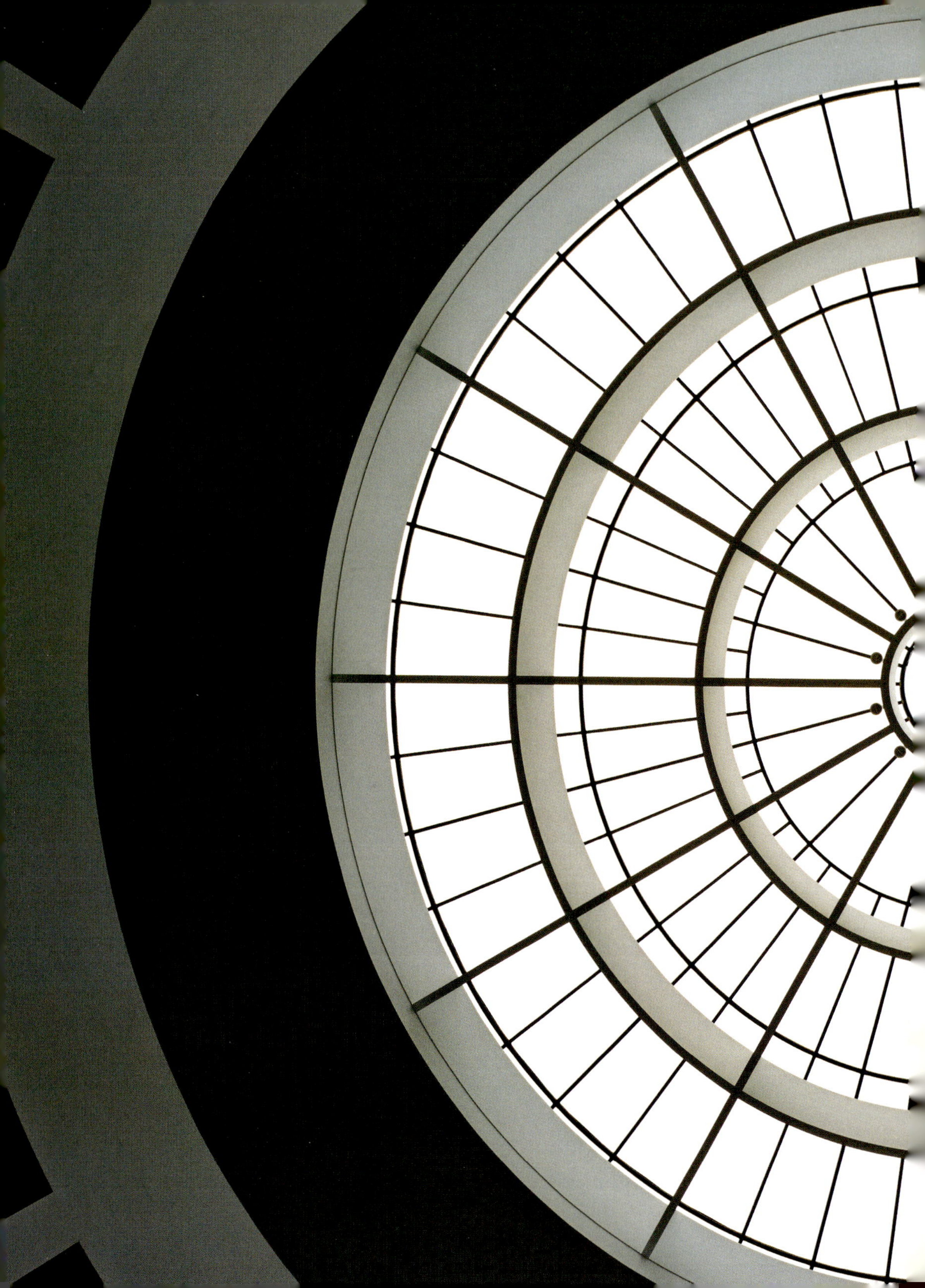

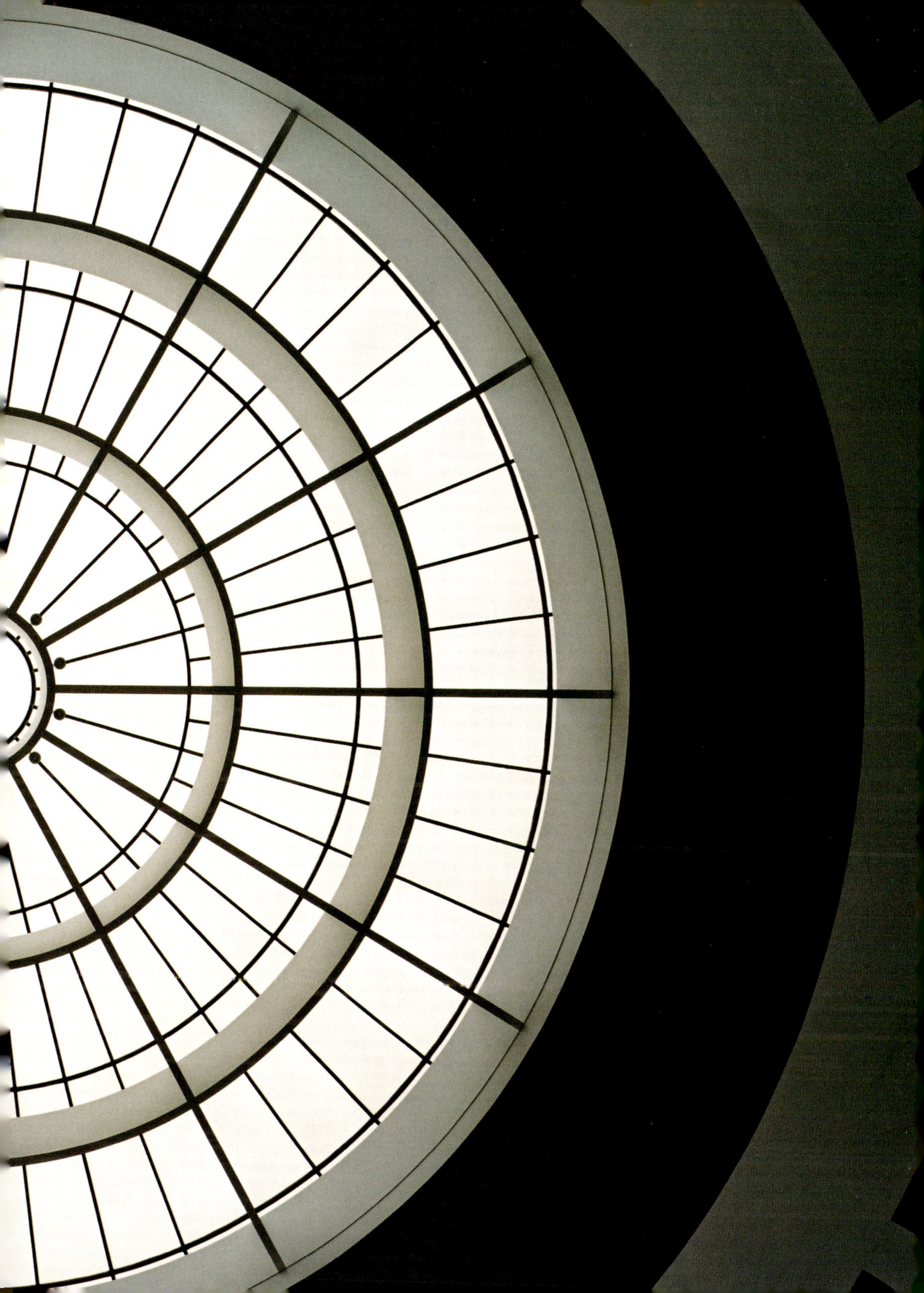

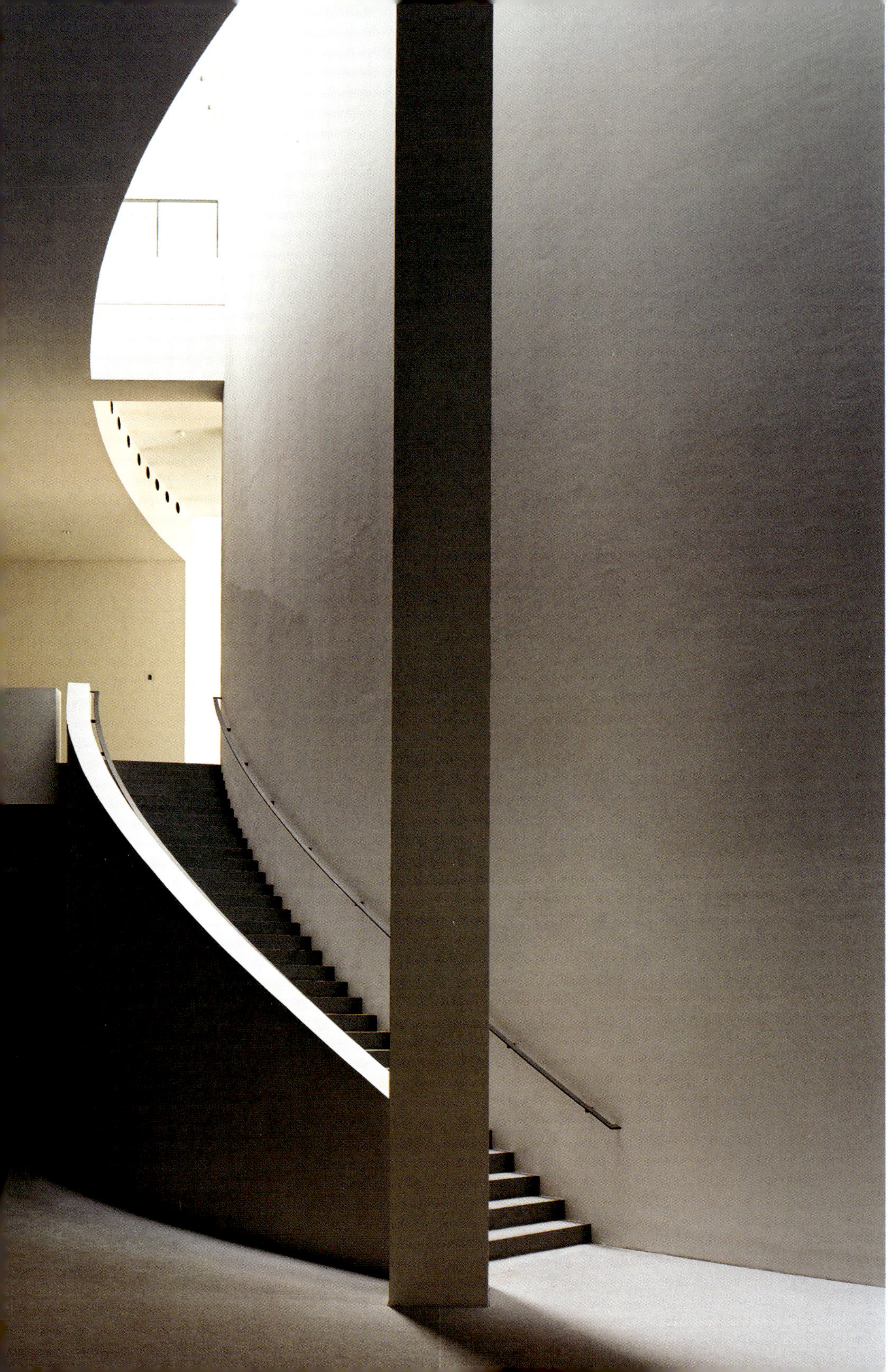

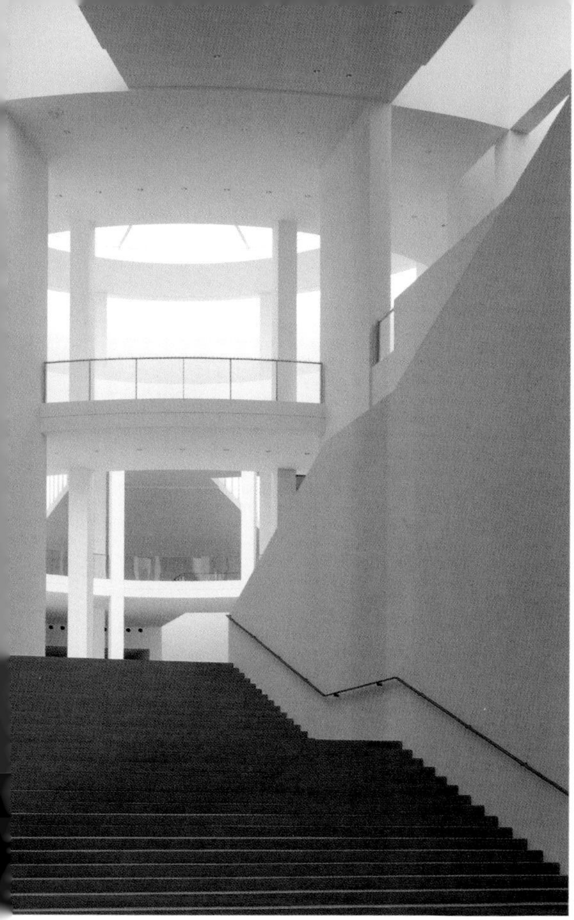

< Treppe ins Untergeschoss Stairway to lower level

Große Diagonaltreppe mit Blick in die Rotunde
Large diagonal stairway with view of rotunda

Turm für den Museumsladen Tower for the museum shop

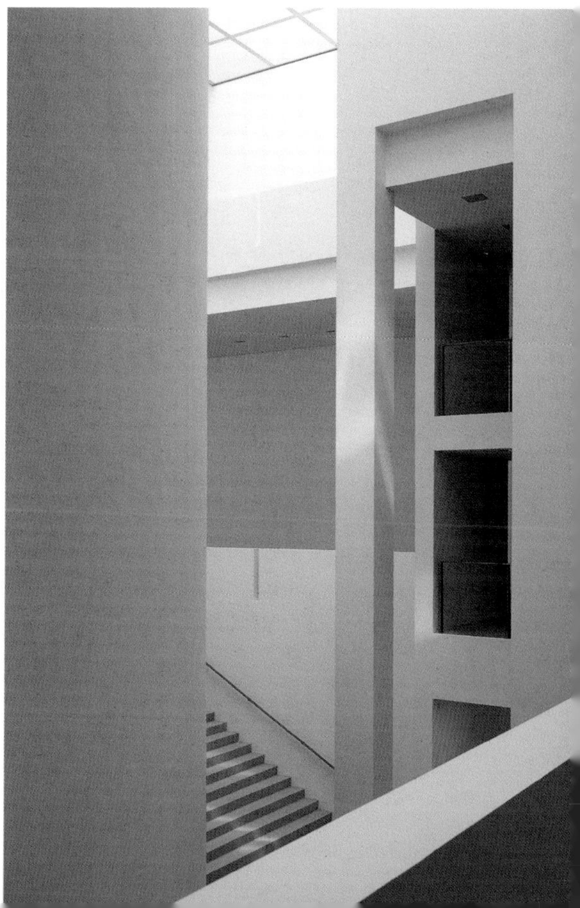

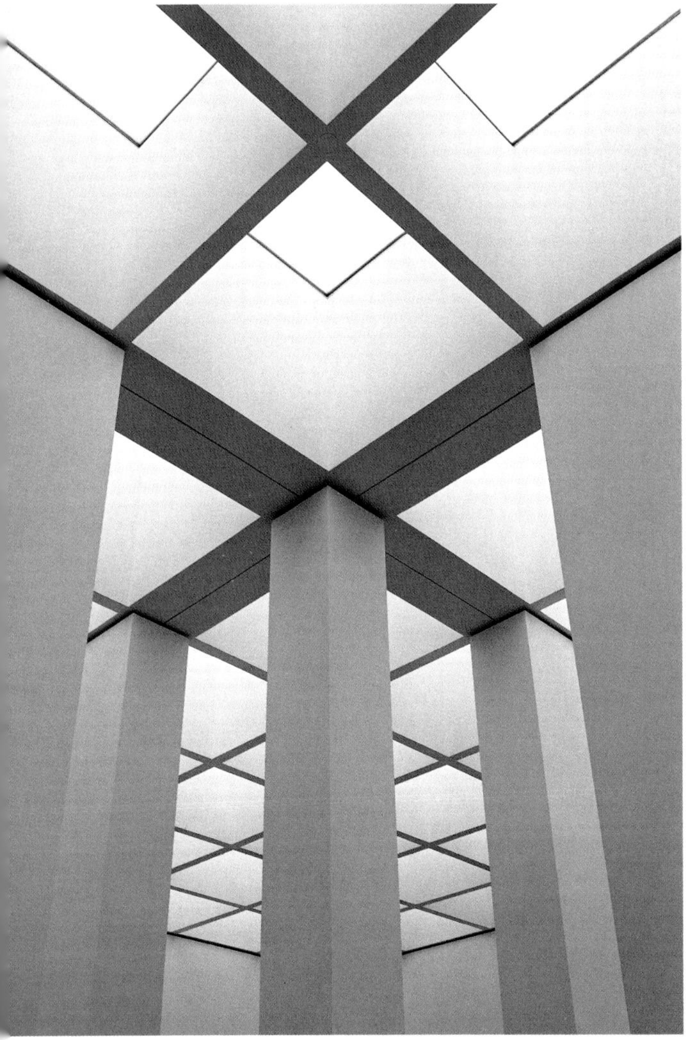

Lichtrasterdecke im Obergeschoss Upper level ceiling

Blick aus einem Ausstellungsraum auf die Rotundenaußenwand
View of outer rotunda wall from an exhibition area

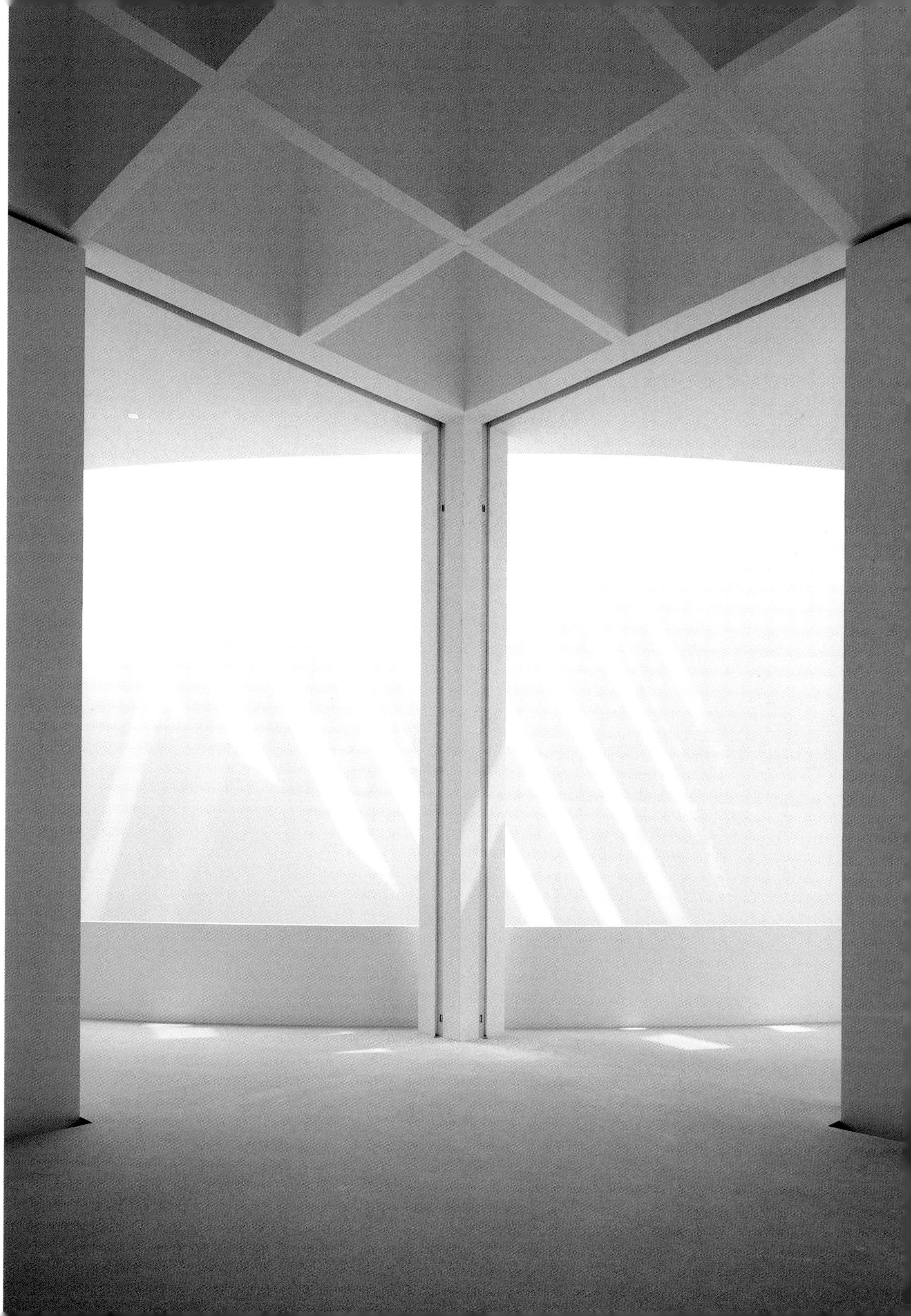

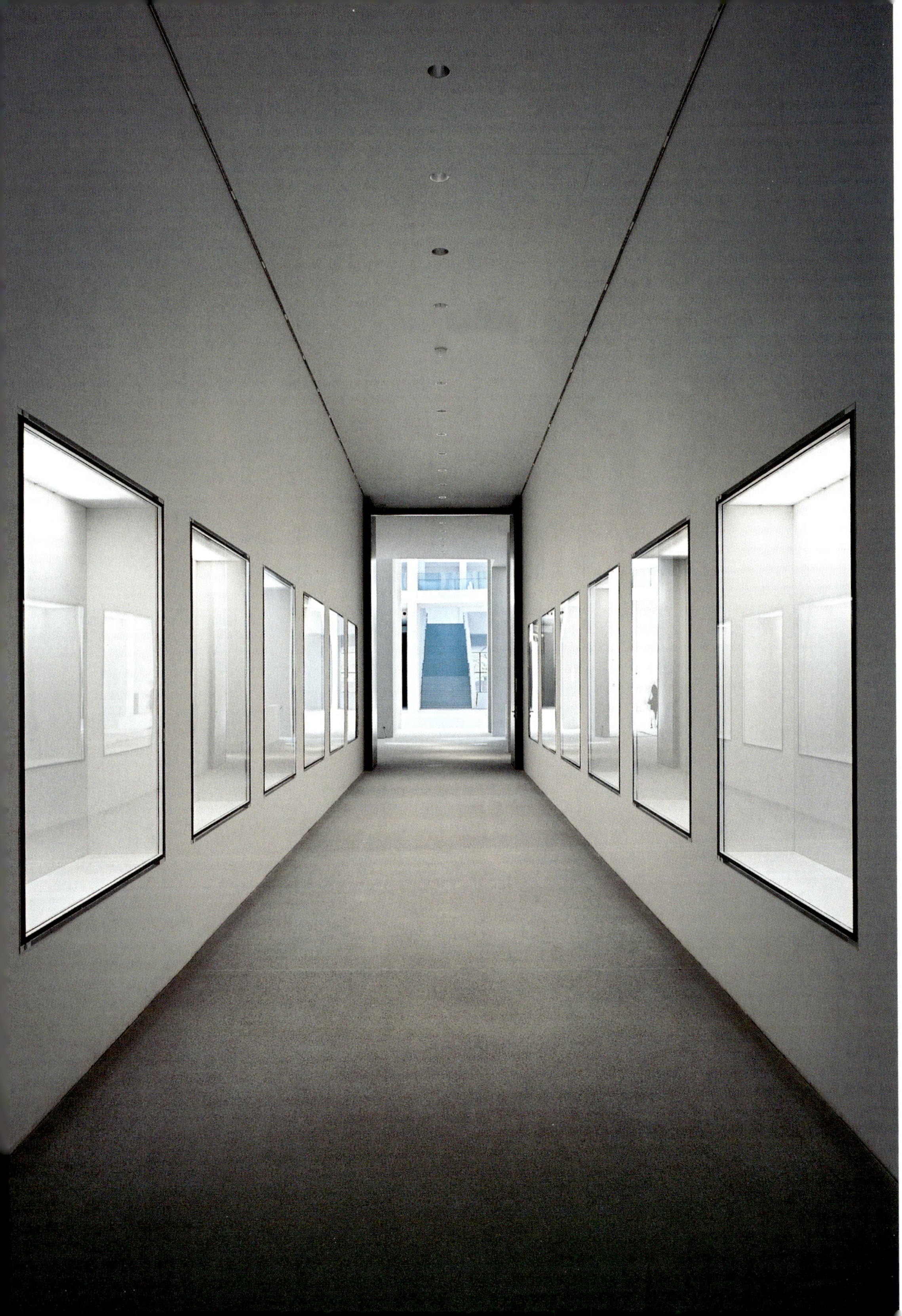

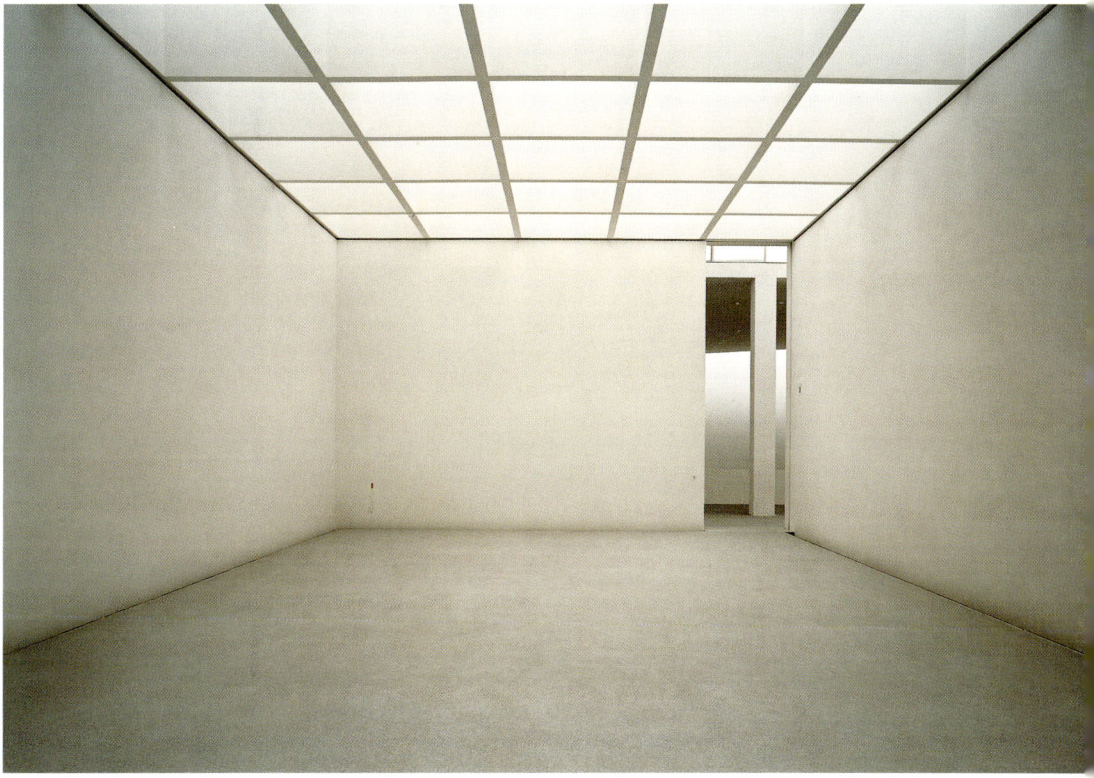

Vitrinengalerie im Erdgeschoss Showcases on the ground floor

Ausstellungssaal im Obergeschoss Upper floor exhibition hall

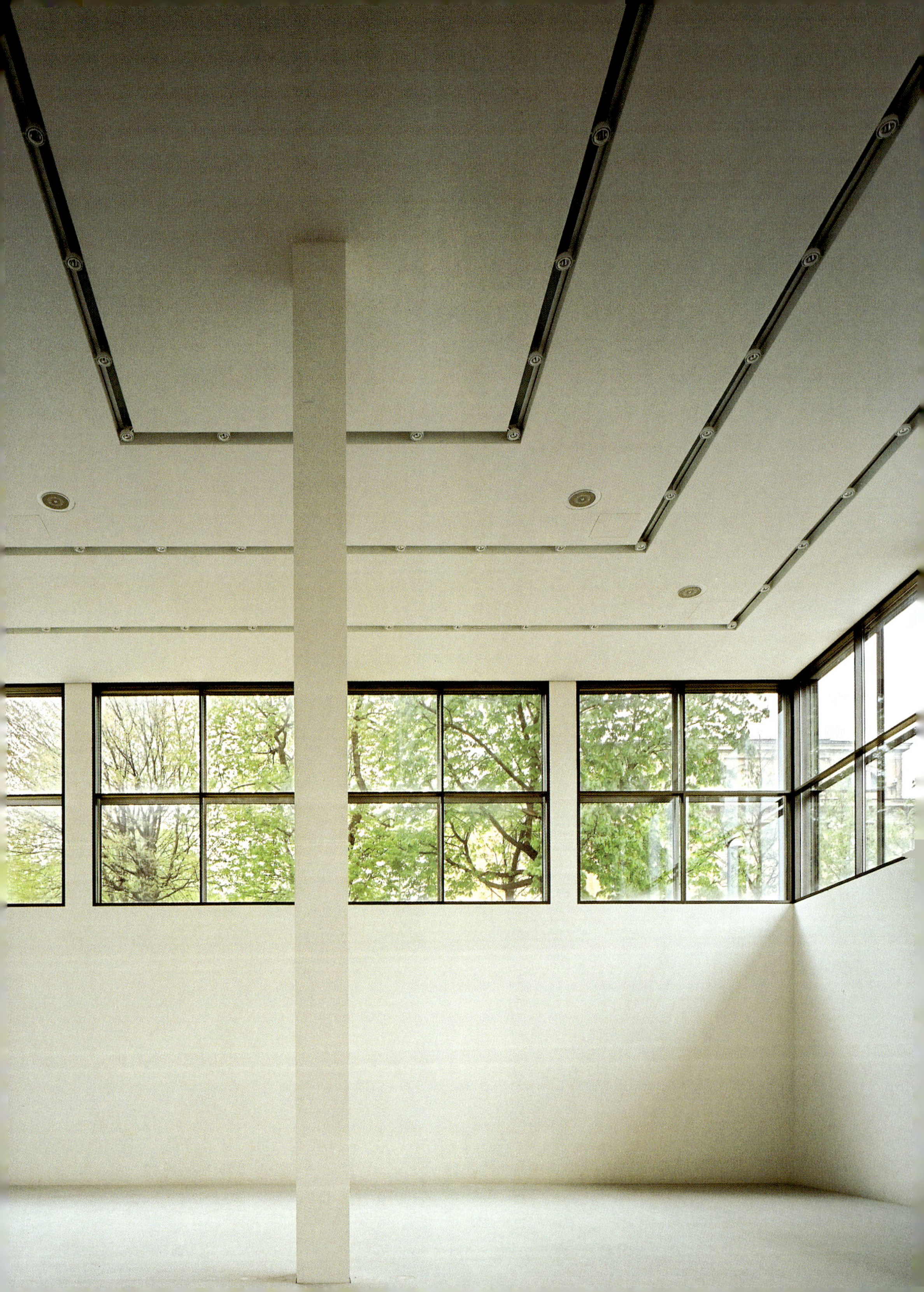

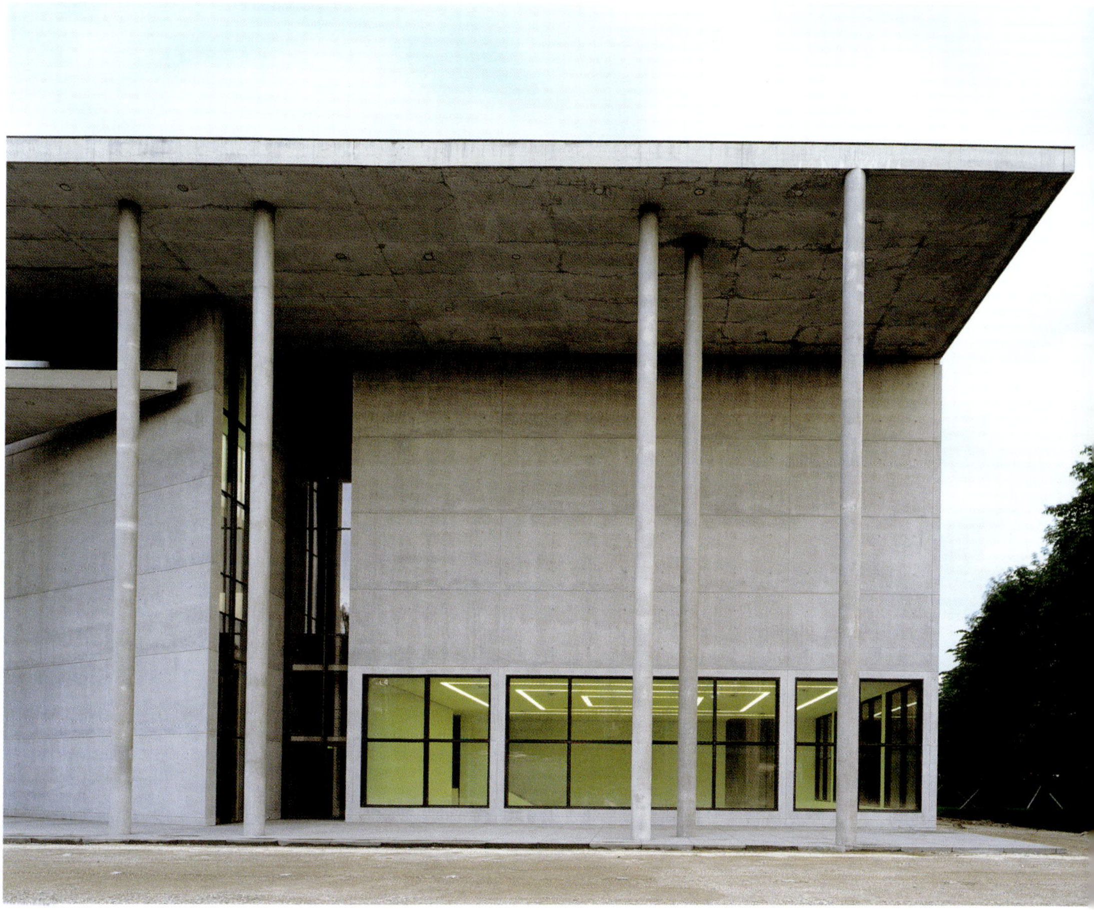

Blick aus dem Großen Saal auf die Alte Pinakothek The Alte Pinakothek seen from the main hall

Großer Saal, Außenansicht Main hall, exterior view

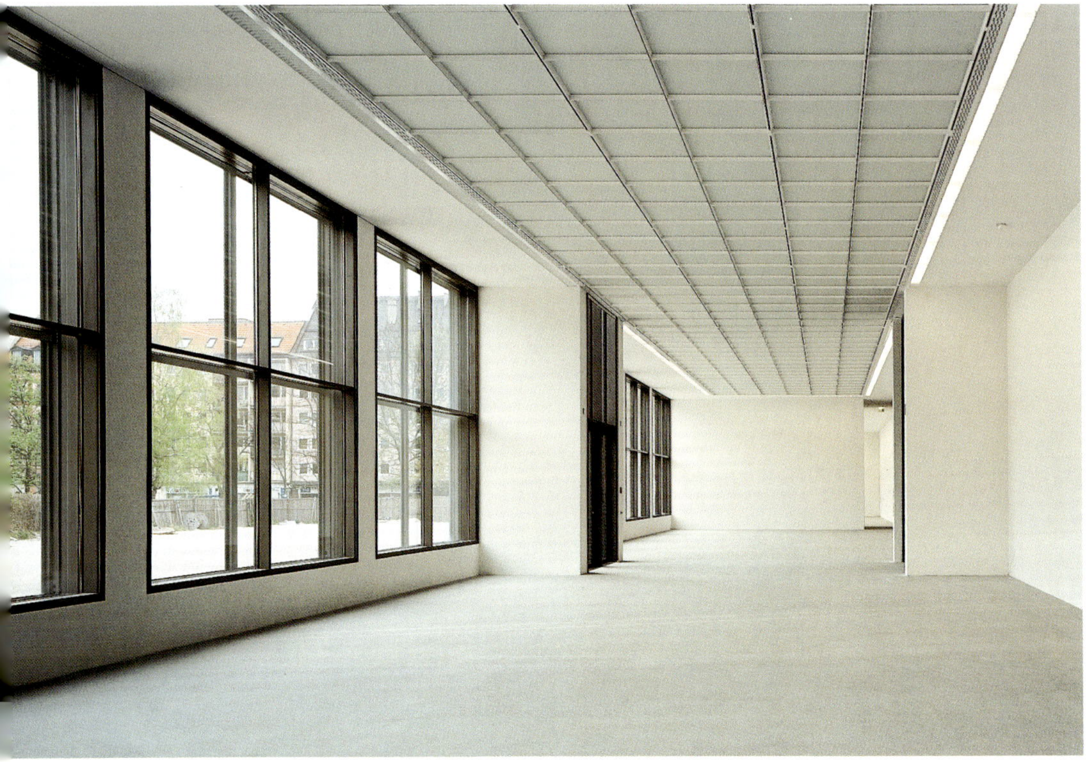

Raumflucht im Erdgeschoss Ground floor rooms

Wintergarten Wintergarden

Blick aus der Eingangsloggia auf die Alte Pinakothek
View of Alte Pinakothek from the entrance loggia >>

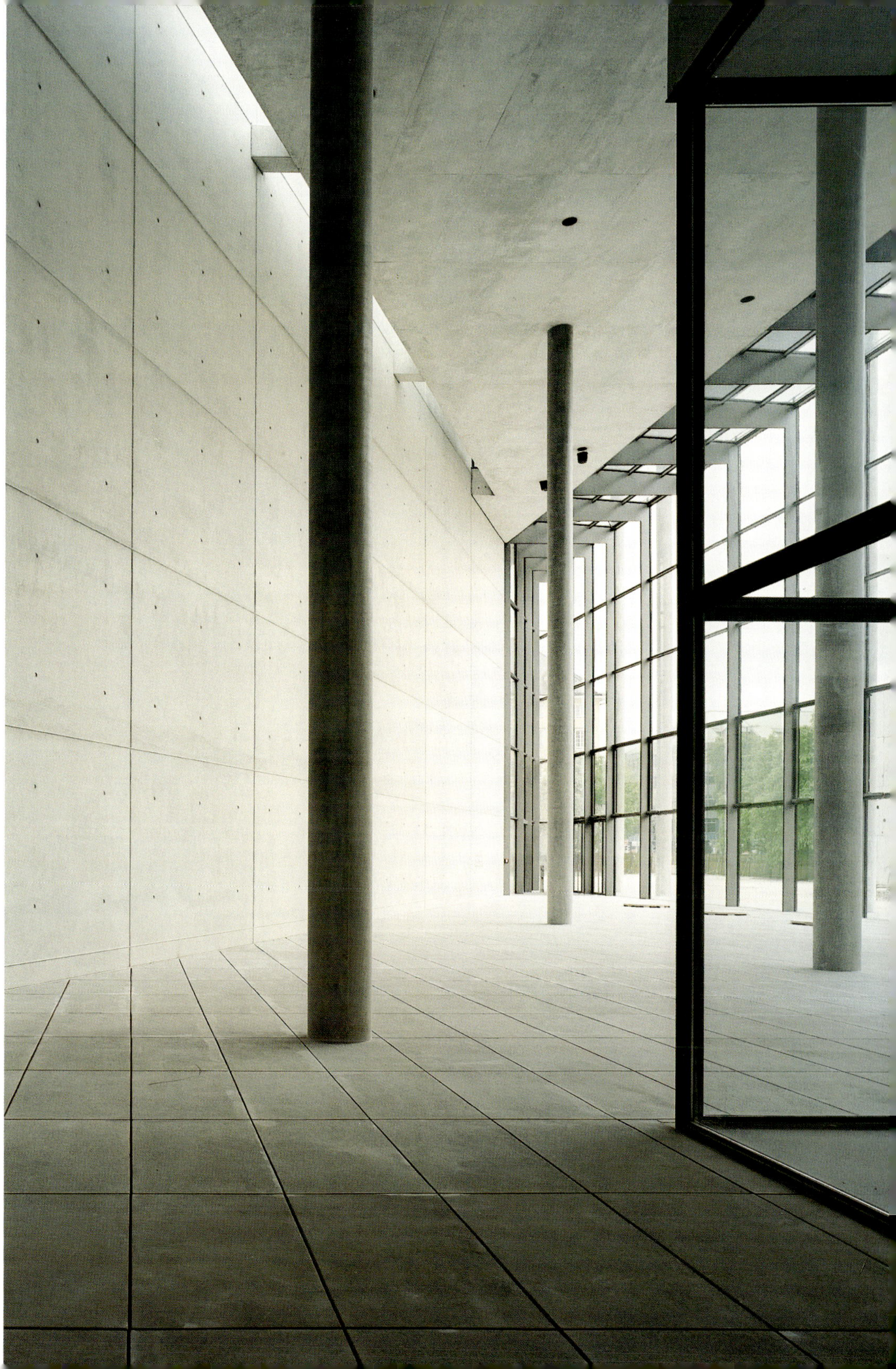

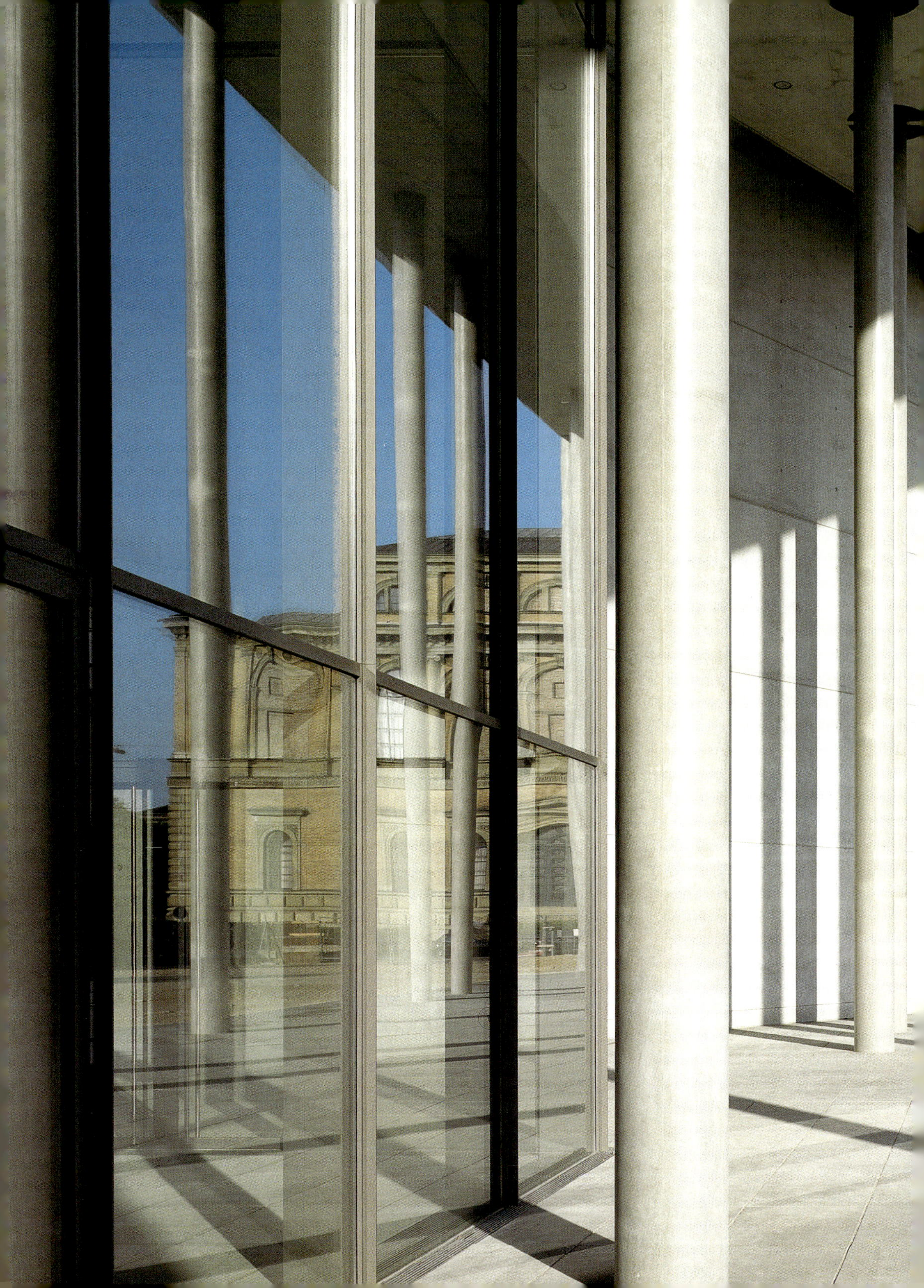

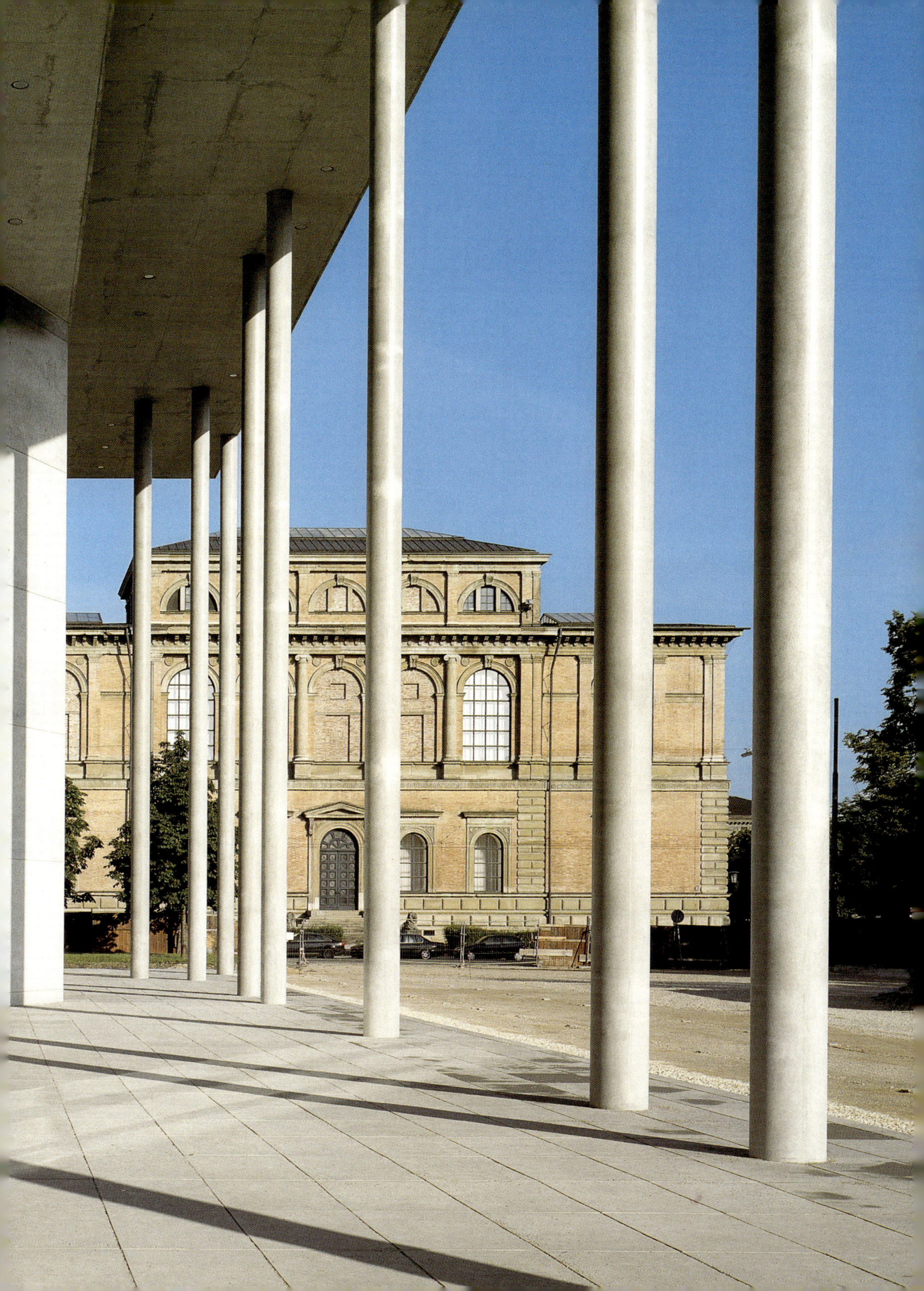

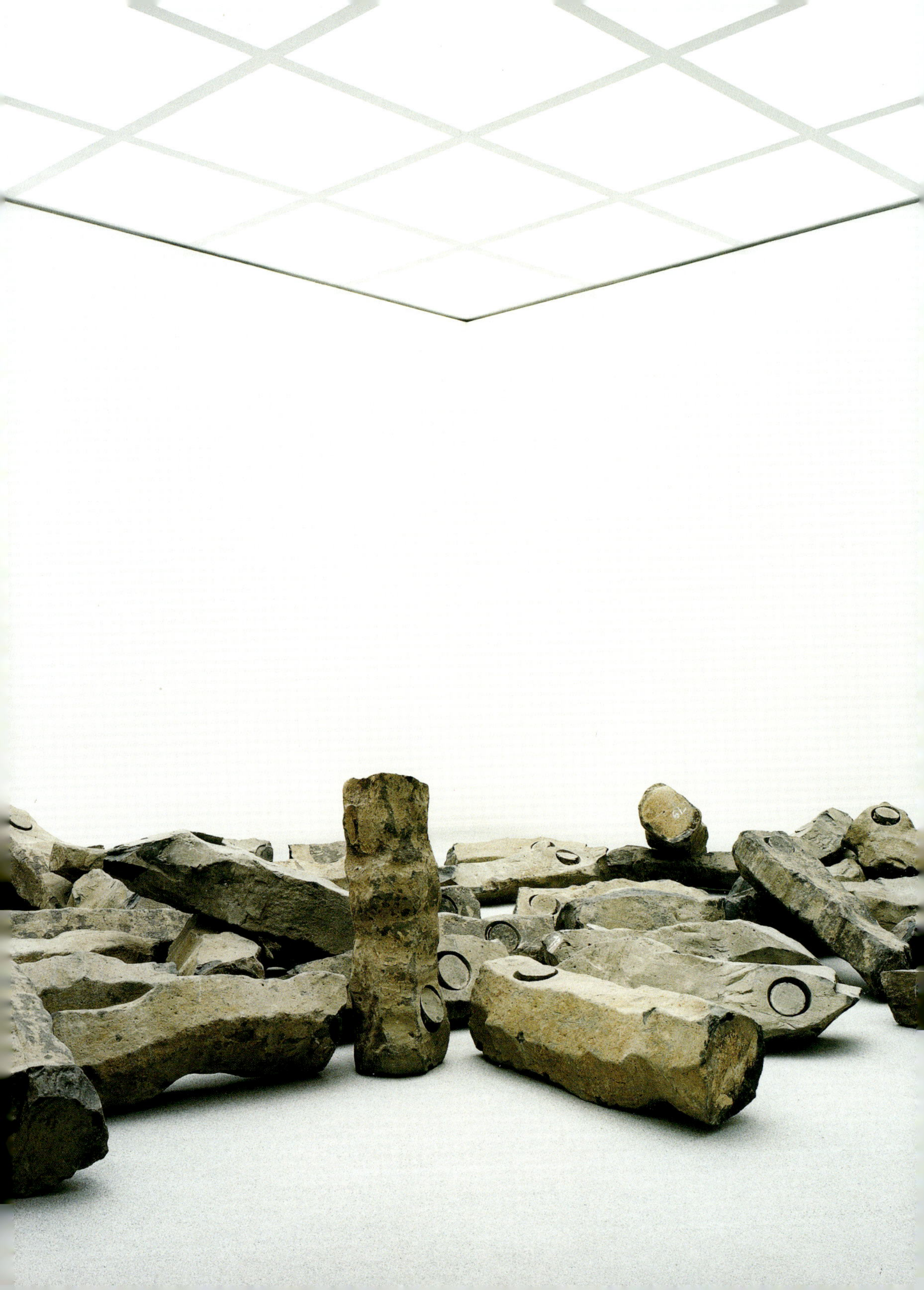

Pinakothek der Moderne
Die Sammlungen The Collections

Staatsgalerie moderner Kunst

Staatliche Graphische Sammlung

Die Neue Sammlung,
Staatliches Museum für angewandte Kunst

Architekturmuseum
der Technischen Universität München

Staatsgalerie moderner Kunst

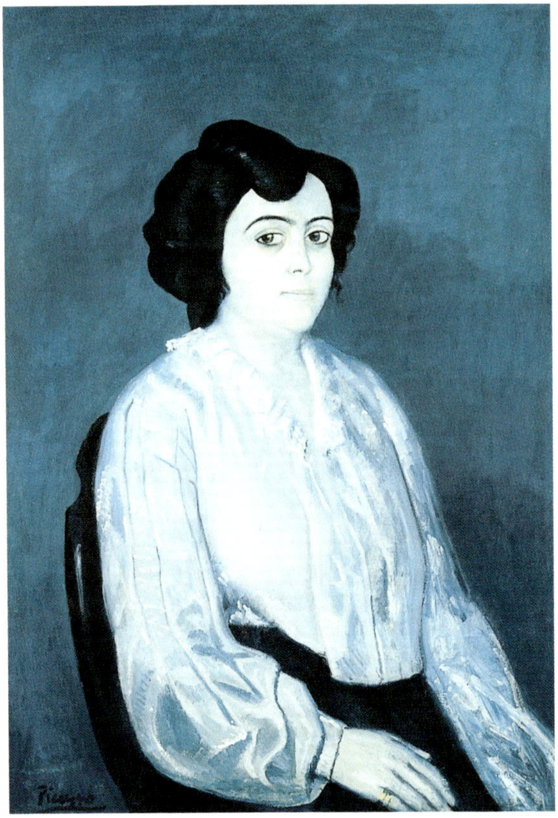

Pablo Picasso, **Madame Soler**, 1903

Im Obergeschoss der Pinakothek der Moderne präsentiert die ehemalige Staatsgalerie moderner Kunst ihre umfangreichen Bestände. Die gesamte Ausstellungsfläche des Stockwerks steht dieser Sammlung herausragender Werke von der klassischen Moderne bis zur zeitgenössischen Kunst zur Verfügung. Erstmals werden hier die Exponate angemessen gezeigt – bislang musste sich die Sammlung auf ein Provisorium im Westflügel des Hauses der Kunst beschränken.

Die Bestände der Staatsgalerie, die nach dem Ersten Weltkrieg als Museum für Gegenwartskunst unter dem Namen ›Neue Staatsgalerie‹ aus der Neuen Pinakothek hervorgegangen war, umfassen bedeutende Einzelwerke sowie Werkgruppen der verschiedenen modernen Kunstströmungen. Innerhalb der klassischen Moderne stellen Gemälde von Künstlern der ›Brücke‹ und des ›Blauen Reiters‹ – etwa von Kirchner, Kandinsky, Klee, Marc oder Macke – einen wichtigen Themenkomplex dar. Herausragend ist die Max-Beckmann-Sammlung; auch Picasso ist mit bedeutenden Gemälden vertreten. Das Umfeld bilden Werke des Kubismus, Futurismus, Bauhaus und Konstruktivismus. Der Surrealismus stellt mit Meisterwerken aus der Theo-Wormland-Stiftung einen weiteren Schwerpunkt dar. Die amerikanische Kunst der Nachkriegszeit ist mit Werken des Abstrakten Expressionismus und der Pop Art reich vertreten; ebenso sind die neueren figurativen Tendenzen und die deutsche Kunst seit den 60er Jahren mit Baselitz, Polke, Kiefer, Lüpertz, Richter und Beuys Sammlungsbestandteil. Die Entwicklung innerhalb der neuen Medien wird anhand prominenter Vertreter anschaulich – etwa mit den Arbeiten von Jeff Wall, einem Environment von George Segal oder Videoinstallationen von Bruce Nauman, Gary Hill und Bill Viola.

<< Joseph Beuys, **Das Ende des 20. Jahrhunderts** **The End of the 20th Century**, 1983

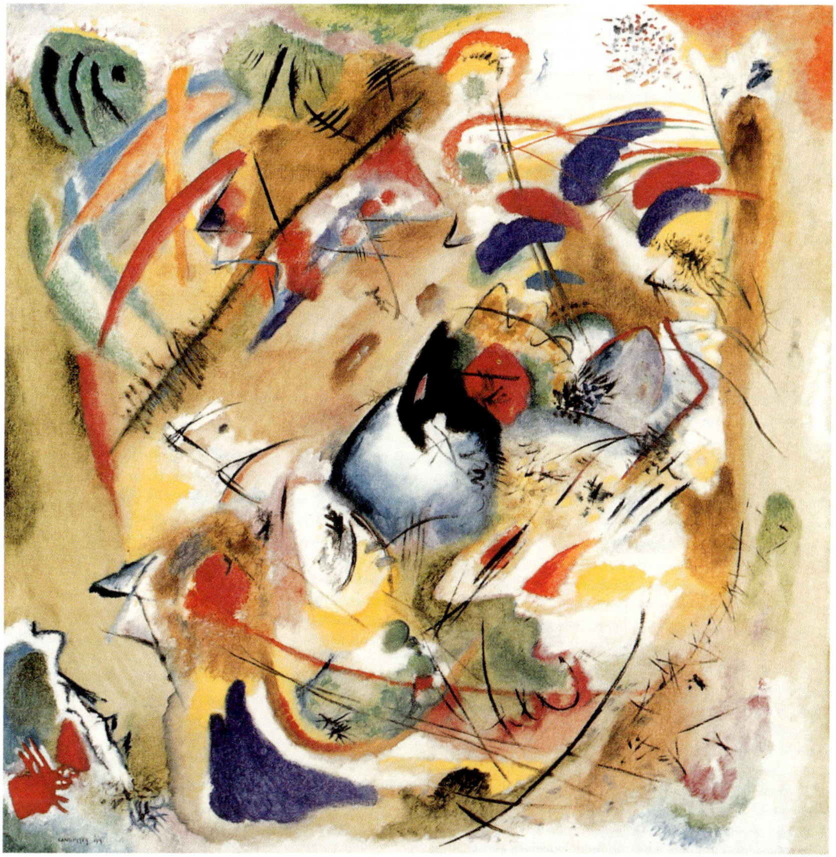

Wassily Kandinsky, **Träumerische Improvisation** **Dream Improvisation**, 1913

The upper floor of the Pinakothek der Moderne houses the collection of the former Staatsgalerie moderner Kunst. The entire exhibition area on this level is dedicated to outstanding works ranging from classical modernism to contemporary art. For the first time, these works can now be shown in an appropriate setting, having previously been restricted to a provisional domicile in the west wing of the building.

The collection, which was founded after the First World War as a museum of contemporary art under the name of Neue Staatsgalerie, based on the holdings of the Neue Pinakothek, brings together important individual works and groups of works from the various movements in modern art. Works by the artists of the Brücke and the Blue Rider—including Kirchner, Kandinsky, Klee, Marc and Macke—are a major component of the Classical Modern section. The Max Beckmann collection is outstanding, and there are several important works by Picasso. In addition, Cubism, Futurism, Bauhaus and Constructivism are all well represented. Surrealism forms a further focal point with masterpieces from the Theo Wormland Foundation. There is a fine selection of postwar American art, from Abstract Expressionism to Pop Art, as well as more recent figurative trends and German art since the 1960s, including works by Baselitz, Polke, Kiefer, Lüpertz, Richter and Beuys. Developments in New Media are portrayed by way of example of Jeff Wall's light boxes, a George Segal environment and video installations by Bruce Nauman, Gary Hill and Bill Viola.

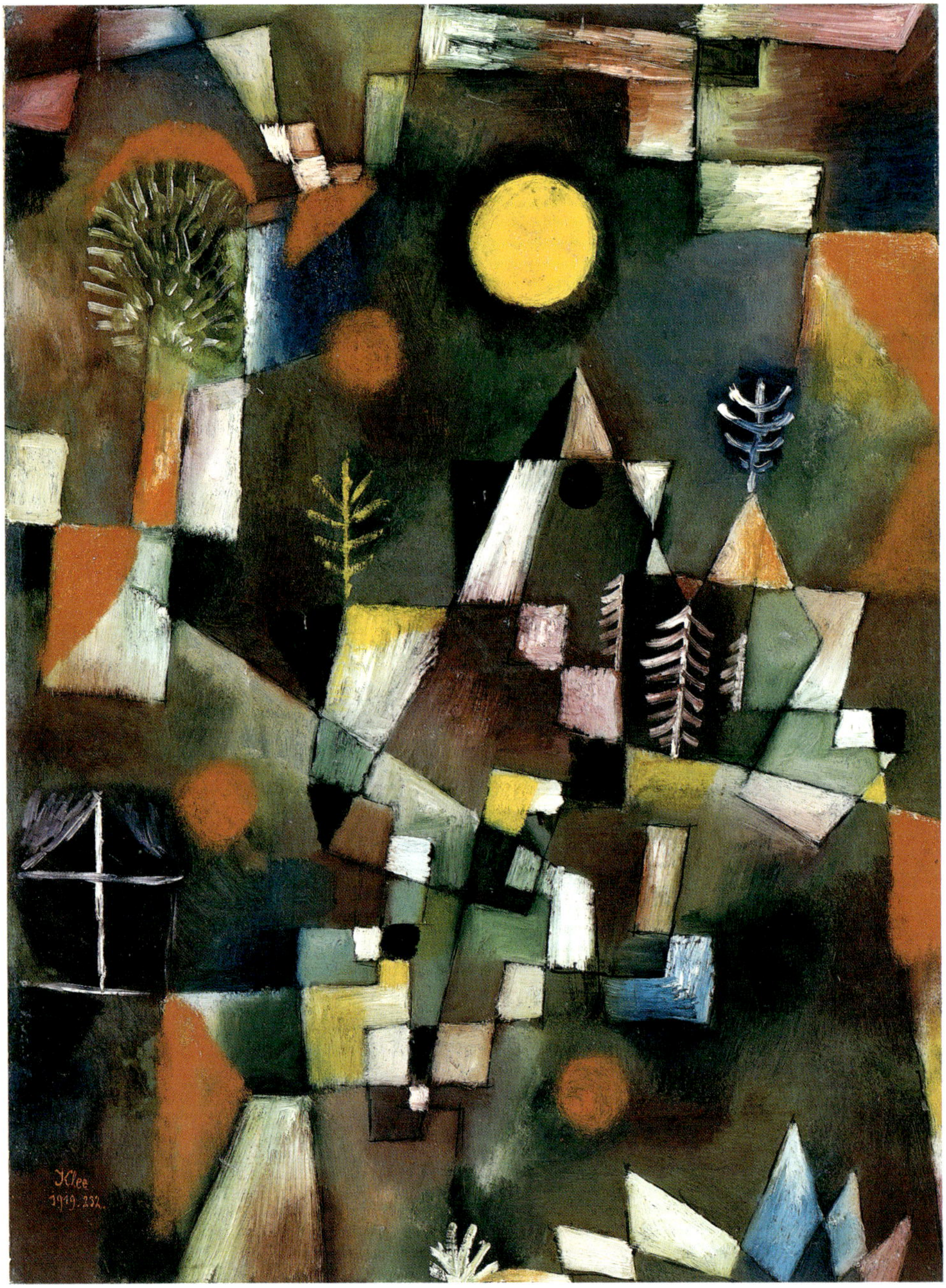

Paul Klee, **Der Vollmond** **Full Moon**, 1919

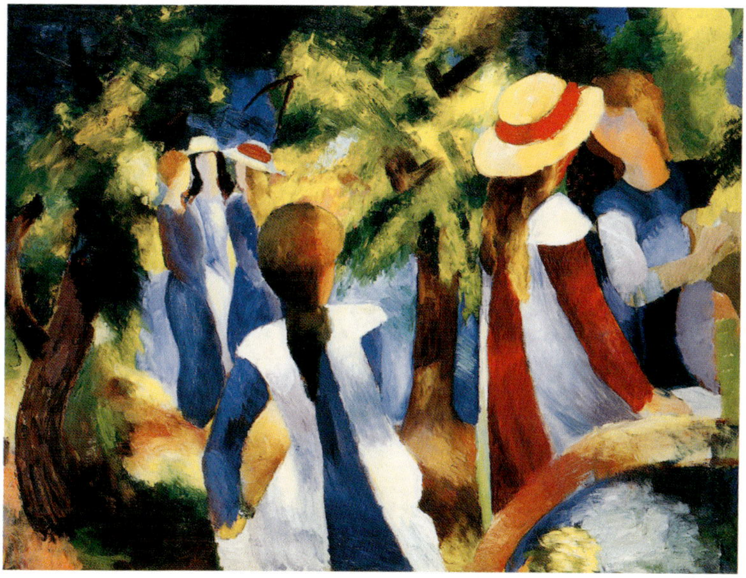

August Macke, **Mädchen unter Bäumen** **Girls under Trees**, 1914

Franz Marc, **Der Mandrill** **The Mandrill**, 1913

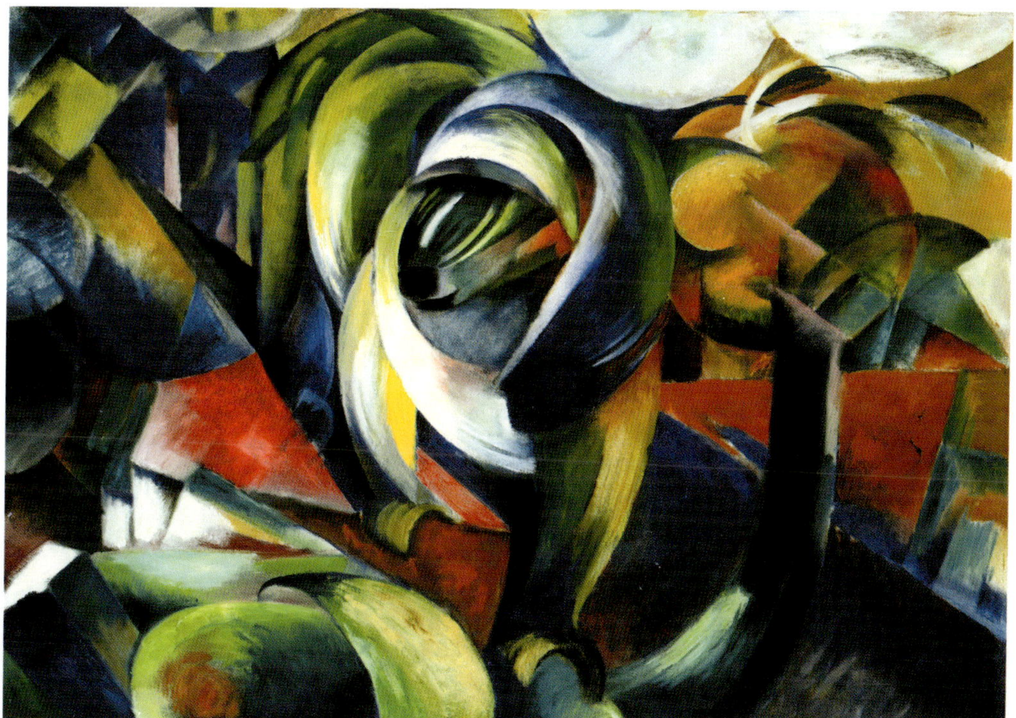

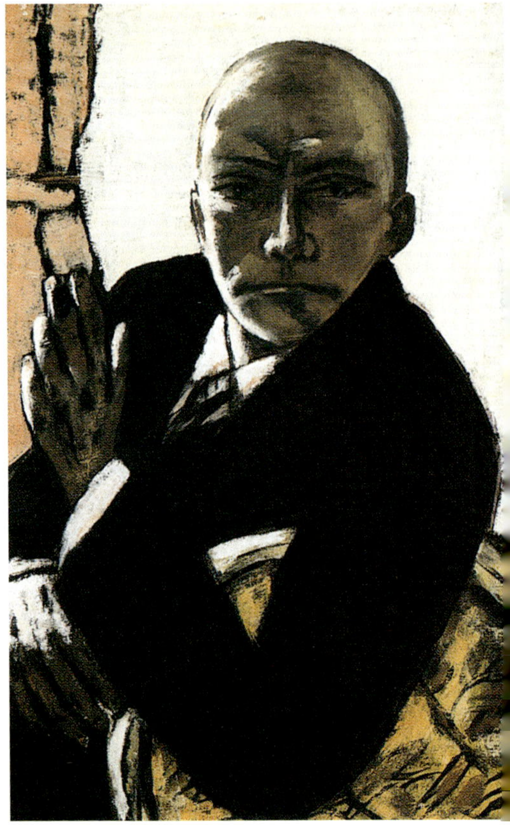

Max Beckmann, **Selbstbildnis** **Self-portrait**, 1944

Giorgio de Chirico, **Selbstbildnis** **Self-portrait**, 1920

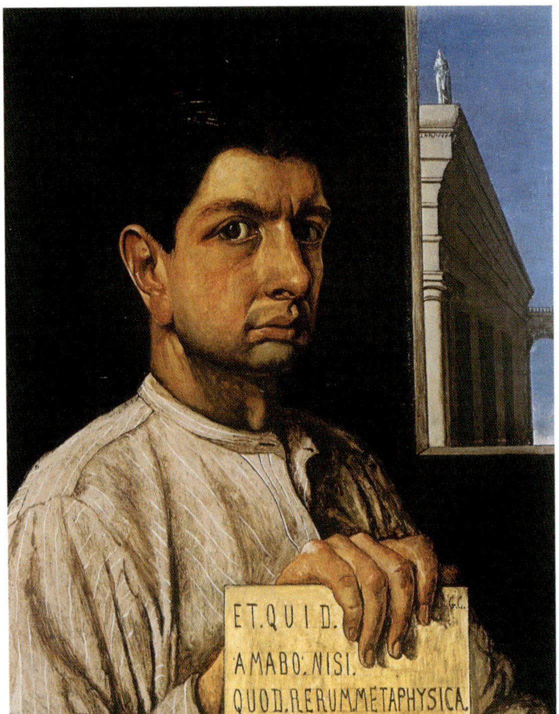

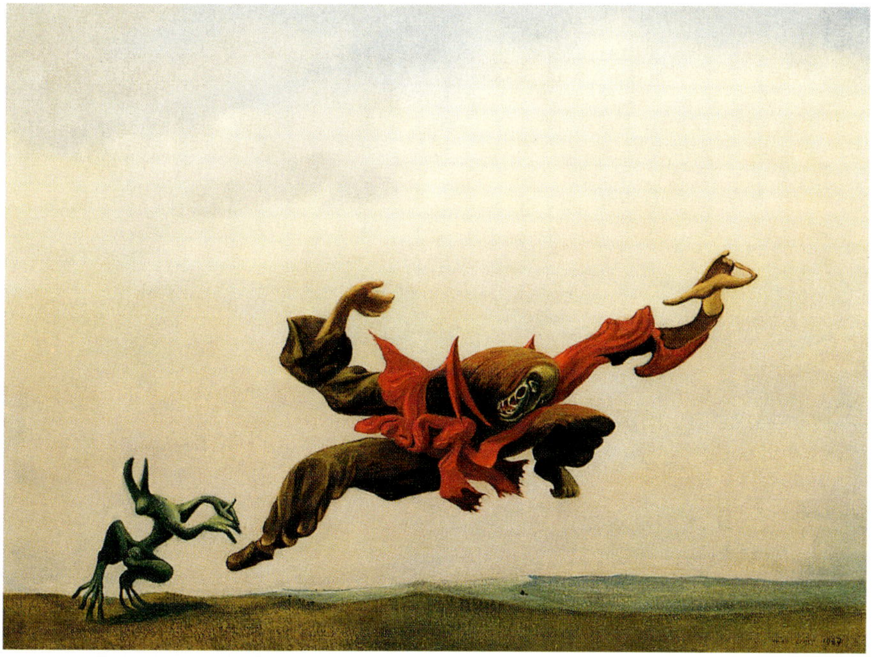

Max Ernst, **Hausengel** **Fireside Angel**, 1937

Salvador Dalí, **Das Rätsel der Begierde** **The Enigma of Desire**, 1929

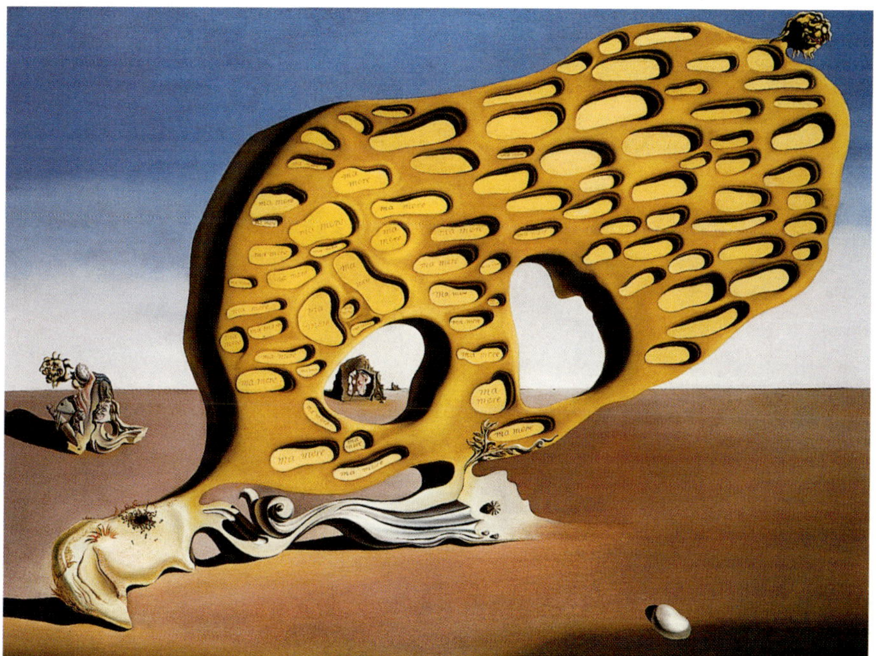

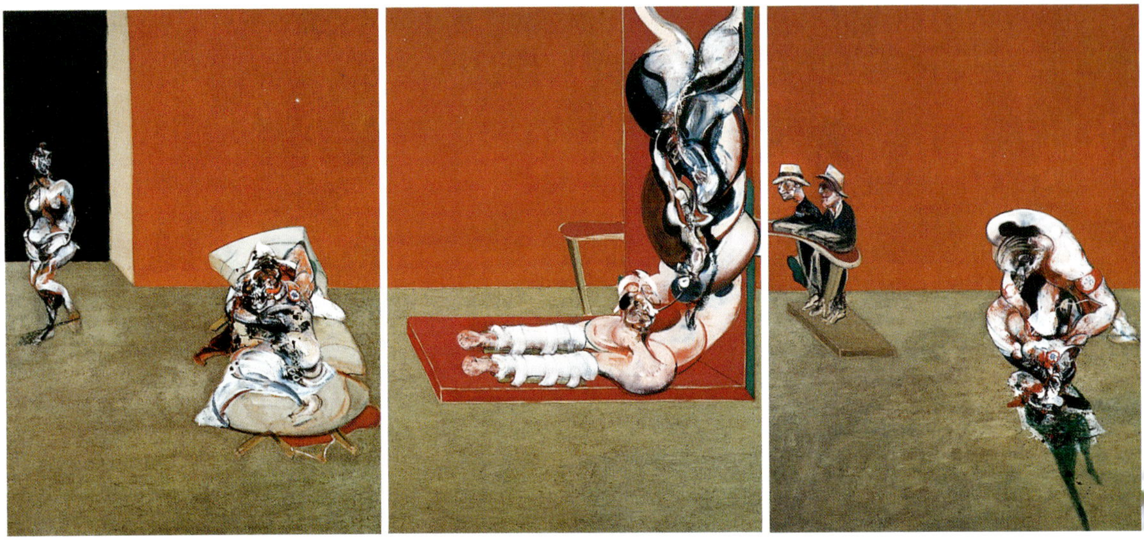

Francis Bacon, **Kreuzigung Crucifixion**, 1965

Jasper Johns, **Arrive/ Depart**, 1963

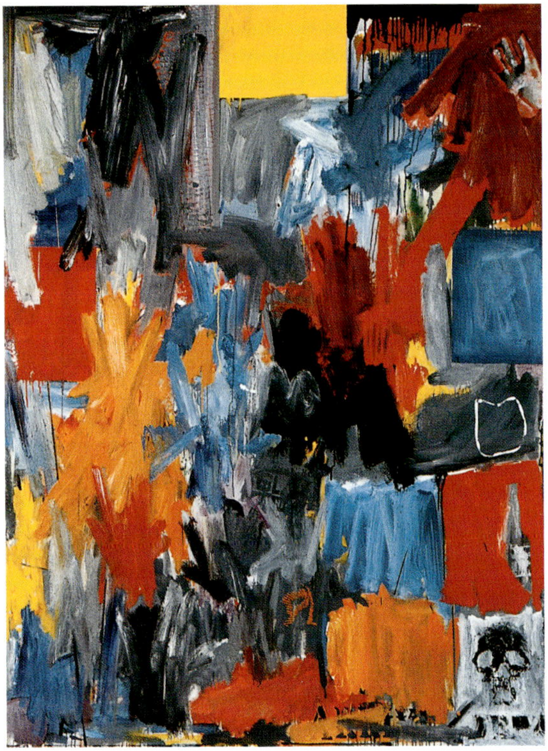

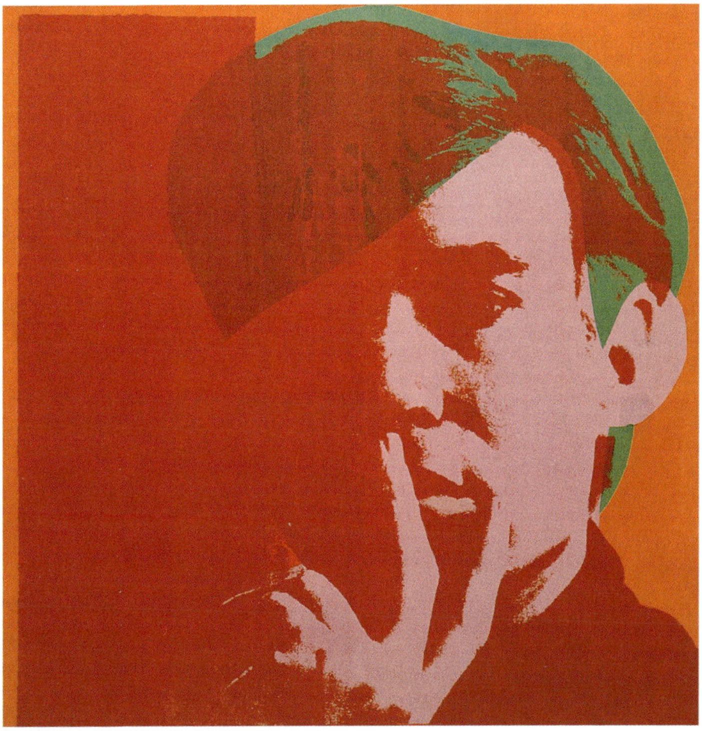

Andy Warhol, **Selbstbildnis**
Self-portrait, 1967

Georg Baselitz, **Der Trommler** **The Drummer**, 1982

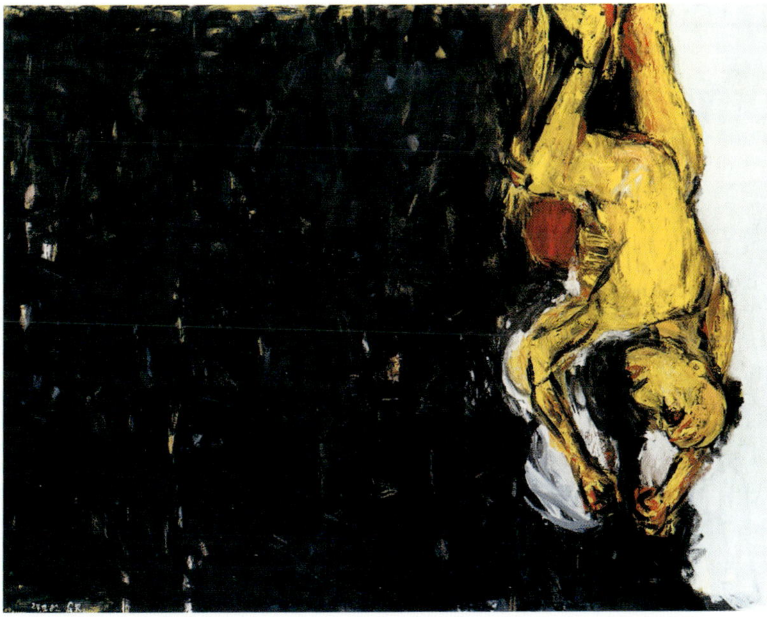

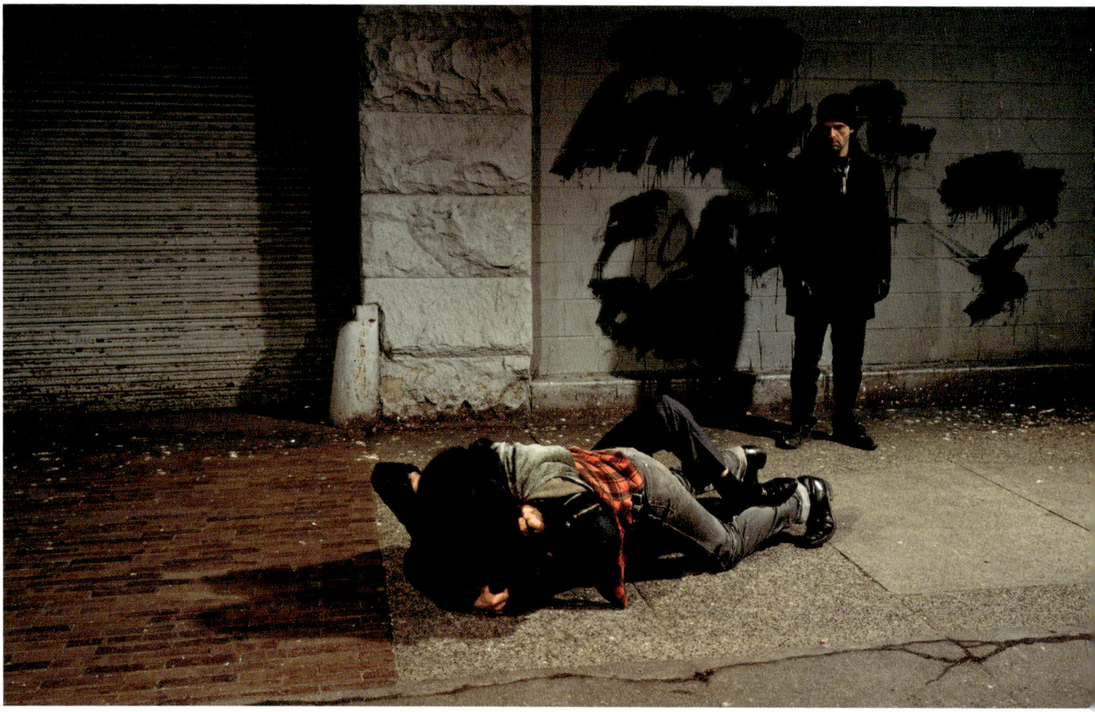

Jeff Wall, **Fight on the Sidewalk**, 1994

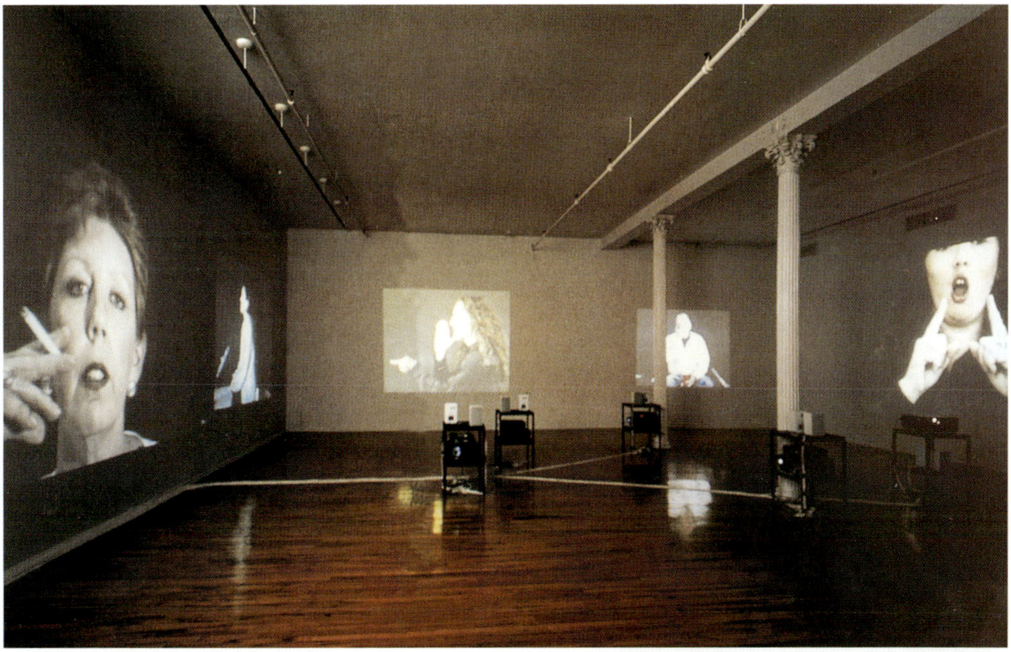

Bruce Nauman, **World Piece Project**, 1996

George Segal, **Alice, ihre Gedichte und Musik hörend** **Alice Listening to her Poems and Music**, 1970

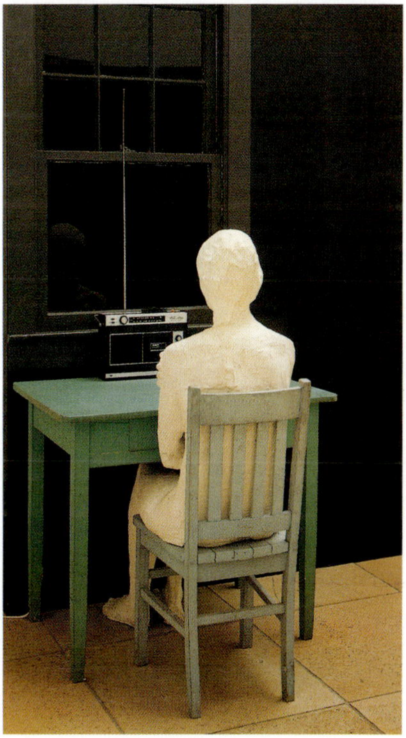

Staatliche Graphische Sammlung

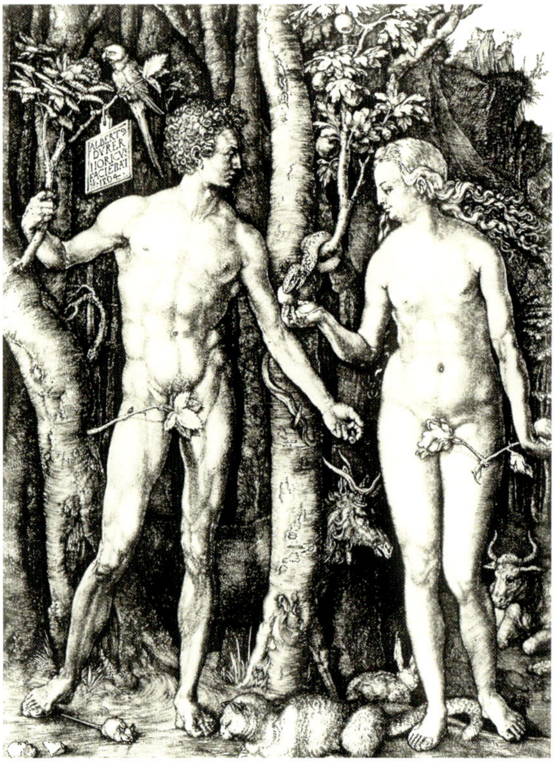

Albrecht Dürer, **Adam und Eva** **Adam and Eve**, 1504

Ständig wechselnde Ausstellungen der Staatlichen Graphischen Sammlung werden im Erdgeschoss der Pinakothek der Moderne präsentiert. Die Sammlung, die kostbare Druckgrafiken und Künstlerzeichnungen vom 15. Jahrhundert bis in die Gegenwart beinhaltet, gehört zu den bedeutendsten Sammlungen der grafischen Künste in Deutschland und ist auch international von hohem Rang. Die Bestände an Zeichungen und Druckgrafiken umfassen über 400000 Blätter und reichen von Leonardo da Vinci über die klassische Moderne bis hin zur zeitgenössischen Grafik. Sammlungsschwerpunkte bilden u.a. frühe Kupferstiche und Einblattholzschnitte, altdeutsche und niederländische Grafik, italienische Renaissancezeichnungen, deutsche Zeichnungen der Romantik sowie die Grafik der klassischen Moderne und der Gegenwart.

Die umfangreiche Sammlung hatte ihren Sitz ursprünglich in der Alten Pinakothek, später im ehemaligen Bau der Neuen Pinakothek. Nach dem Zweiten Weltkrieg wurde sie auf sehr beengtem Raum in einem ehemaligen Verwaltungsgebäude untergebracht. Neben der Pinakothek der Moderne wird im Zuge des zweiten Bauabschnitts ein eigenes Gebäude entstehen, das der Graphischen Sammlung ihren vielfältigen Anforderungen entsprechende Räumlichkeiten wie Depots, Restaurierungswerkstätten, einen Seminarraum und einen Studiensaal bietet.

A continual series of temporary exhibitions featuring works from the Staatliche Graphische Sammlung will be presented on the ground floor of the Pinakothek der Moderne. This internationally renowned collection of magnificent prints and drawings from the fifteenth century to the present day is one of the foremost collections of its kind in Germany. It comprises more than 400,000 works on paper, from Leonardo da Vinci to Classical Modernism and contemporary art. The main focus of the collection is on early copperplate engravings and woodcuts, Old German and Netherlandish prints, Italian Renaissance drawings, German Romantic drawings, Classical Modern and contemporary prints.

This wide-ranging collection was originally housed in the Alte Pinakothek and later moved to the former Neue Pinakothek building. After the Second World War it was kept under somewhat cramped conditions in a former administrative building. The second construction phase will entail erecting a separate building next to the Pinakothek der Moderne that caters to the specific needs of the Graphische Sammlung, providing storage depots, restoration workshops, a seminar room and a study room.

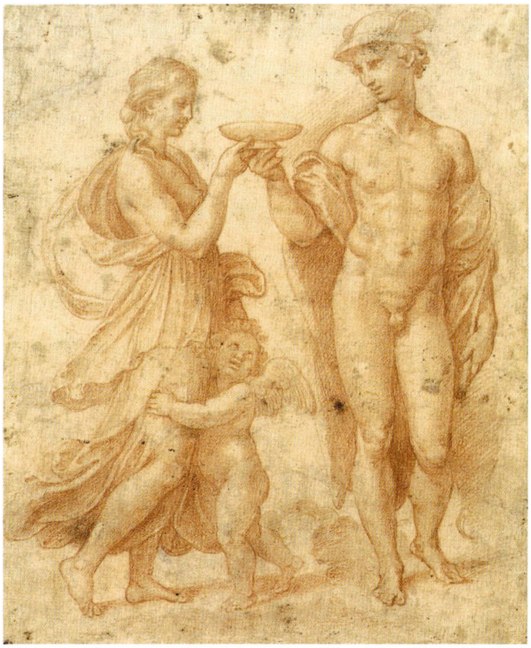

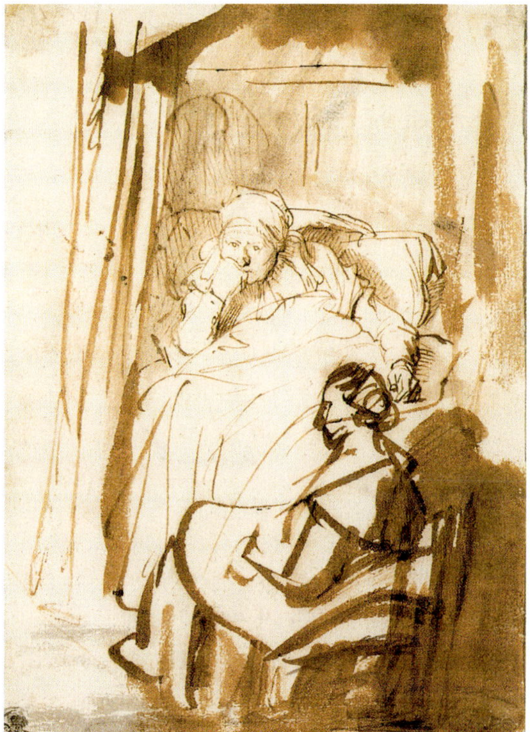

Raffael Raphael, **Merkur reicht Psyche die Schale mit dem Trank der Unsterblichkeit Mercury giving Psyche the Draught of Immortality**, um c. 1517

Rembrandt, **Saskia im Bett mit einer Amme Saskia with a Nurse**, um c. 1638

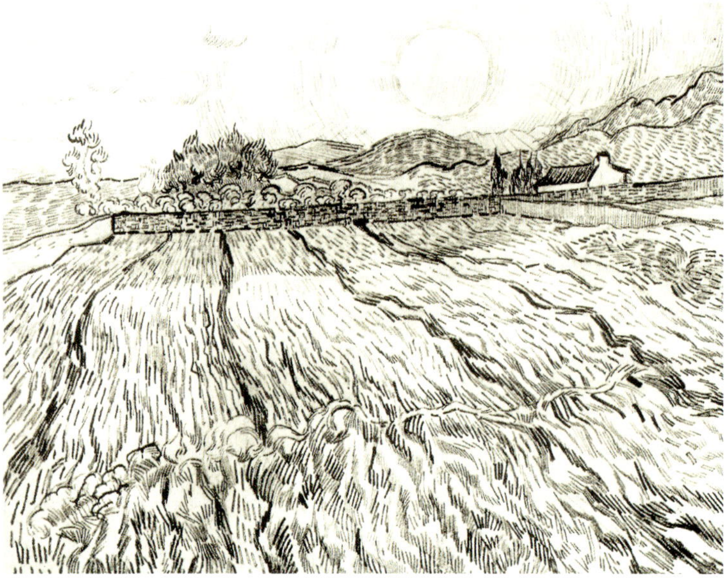

Vincent van Gogh, **Landschaft mit aufgehender Sonne** **Landscape with Rising Sun**, 1889

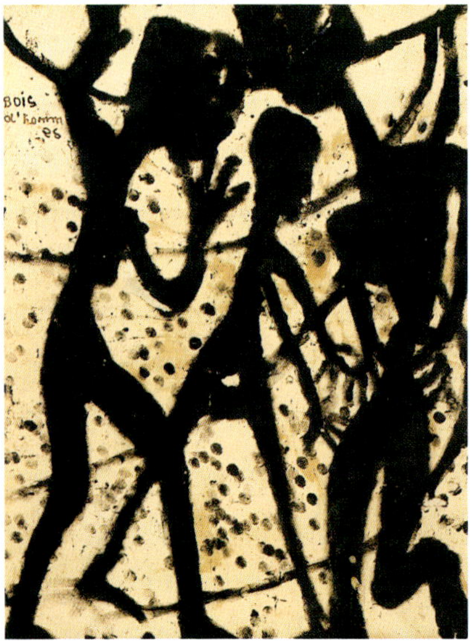

Louis Soutter, **Bois d'hommes**, um c. 1938–42

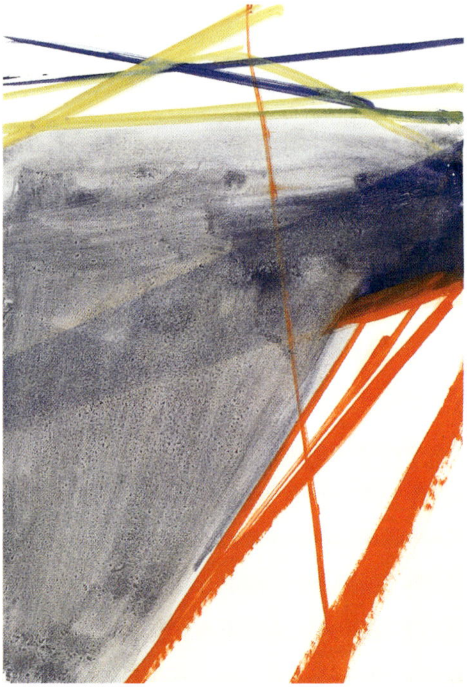

Blinky Palermo, **Die Landung** **The Landing**, 1965

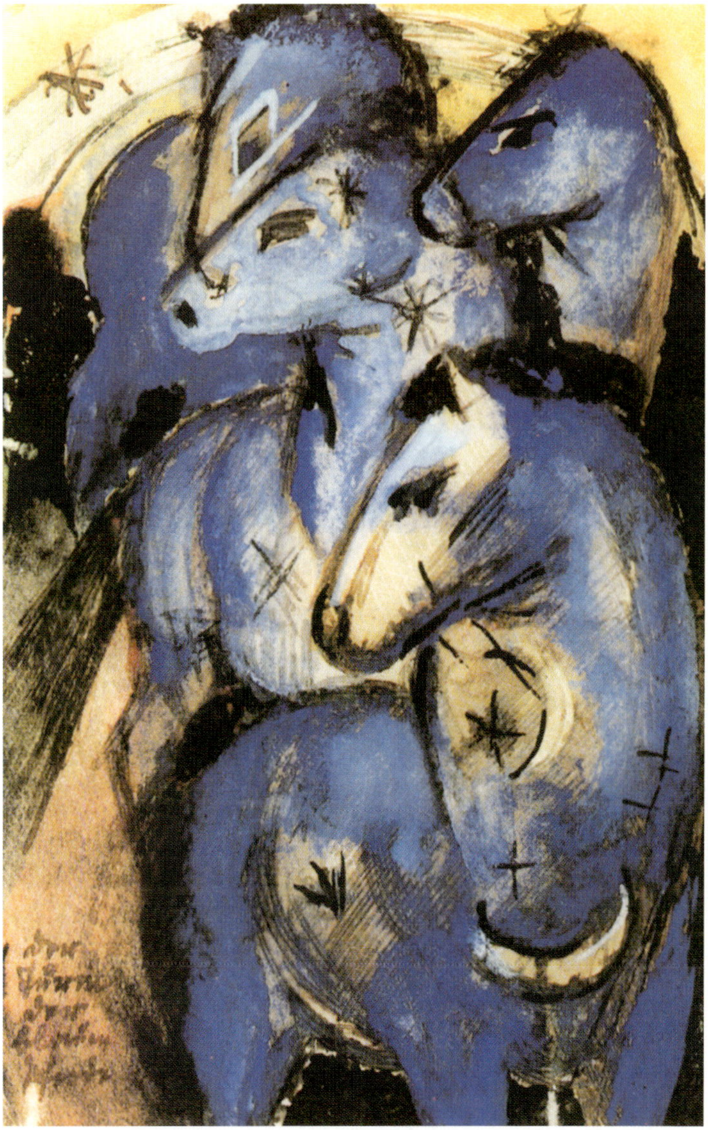

Franz Marc, **Der Turm der blauen Pferde** **The Tower of Blue Horses**, 1912/13

Die Neue Sammlung, Staatliches Museum für angewandte Kunst

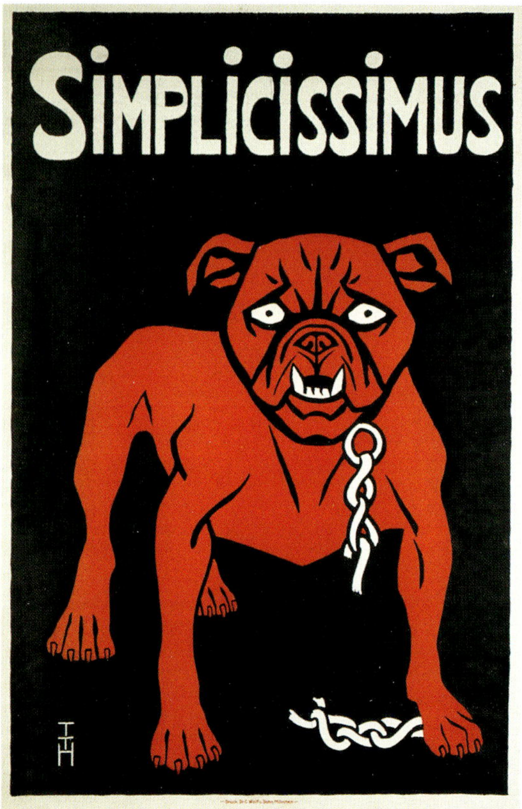

Thomas Theodor Heine, **Plakat für die Zeitschrift ›Simplicissimus‹** **Poster for "Simplicissimus"**, 1897

Das Untergeschoss der Pinakothek der Moderne steht der Neuen Sammlung, die international zu den bedeutendsten Museen für angewandte Kunst gehört, zur Verfügung. Das Museum, das über 60 000 Objekte des internationalen Designs und Kunsthandwerks von 1900 bis zur Gegenwart besitzt, war bisher in einem Annexbau des Bayerischen Nationalmuseums untergebracht und präsentiert nun erstmals dauerhaft und in räumlicher Breite erstrangige Beispiele der Sammlung. Neben Prototypen des Designs aus dem 19. Jahrhundert vereint die Sammlung insbesondere die angewandte Kunst seit der Zeit der industriellen Revolution. Sammlungsschwerpunkte sind die seriell hergestellten Produkte des Industriedesigns – Elektrogeräte, Beleuchtungskörper, Werkzeuge, Motoren, Fahrzeuge, Sportgeräte und Produkte aus dem Gebiet der neuen Medien – sowie die Bereiche des Grafikdesigns mit Plakatkunst, Buchgestaltung oder Fotografie und des Kunsthandwerks. Für die bedeutende Stühlesammlung wurde ein eigener Raum, das Amphitheater in der Rotunde, konzipiert; ebenfalls in einem eigenen Raum wird die herausragende Schmucksammlung der Danner-Stiftung präsentiert. Die Fülle der Exponate wird ein über zwei Geschosse reichendes so genanntes ›begehbares Depot‹ zeigen.

The lower floor of the Pinakothek der Moderne houses the Neue Sammlung, which is one of the world's most important museums of applied art. This museum, with over 60,000 works of international design and applied arts from 1900 to the present day, previously occupied an annexe of the Bayerisches Nationalmuseum. Now, for the first time, the finest pieces of this collection can be placed on permanent display in a broader setting. Apart from nineteenth-century design prototypes, the collection brings together examples of applied arts since the Industrial Revolution. The focus of the collection is on serially manufactured industrial design—electrical appliances, lamps, tools, motors, vehicles, sports equipment and new media products—and on graphic design, including posters, typography, photography and craftsmanship. The amphitheatre in the rotunda was specially created for the important collection of chairs. The superb jewellery collection of the Danner Foundation is also presented in a room of its own. The wealth of exhibits will be displayed in an over two-storey high "walk-in depot".

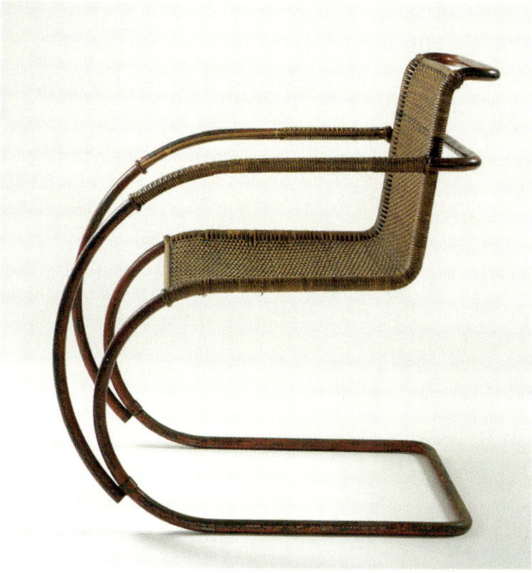

Ludwig Mies van der Rohe, **Freischwingerstuhl ›MR 20‹**
Cantilever chair "MR 20", 1927

Otto Wagner, **Schreibtisch und Hocker der Wiener Postsparkasse**
Writing desk and stool for Vienna Post Office Savings Bank, 1906

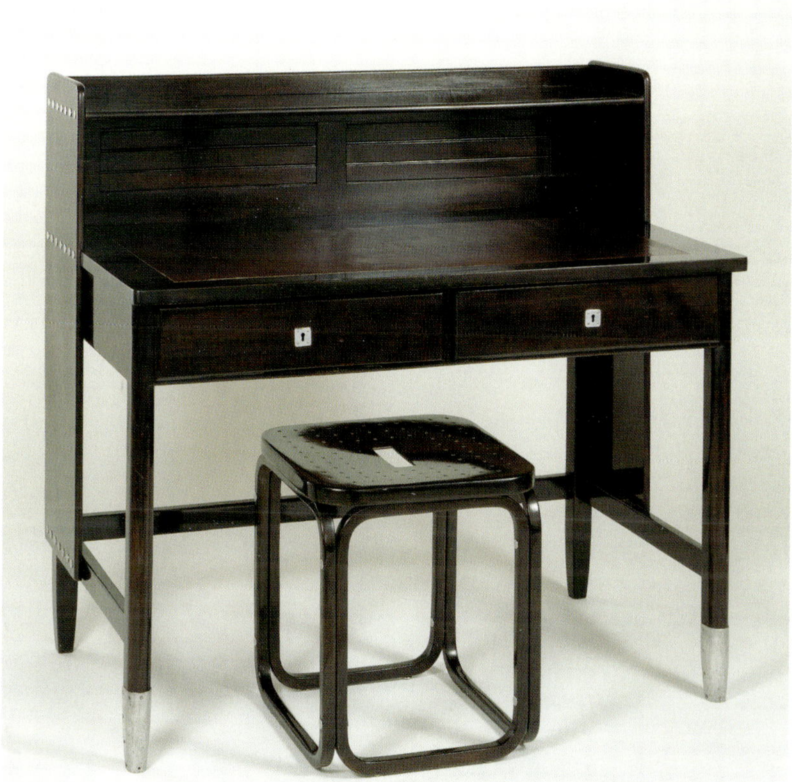

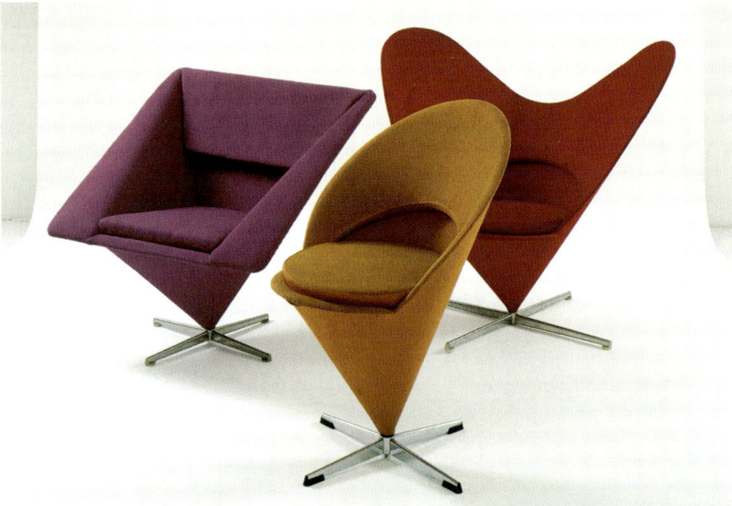

Verner Panton, **Sessel Armchair**, 1960; ›**Cone Chair**‹, 1958; ›**Mickey Mouse**‹, 1959

Hans Ledwinka, **Tatra 87**, 1937

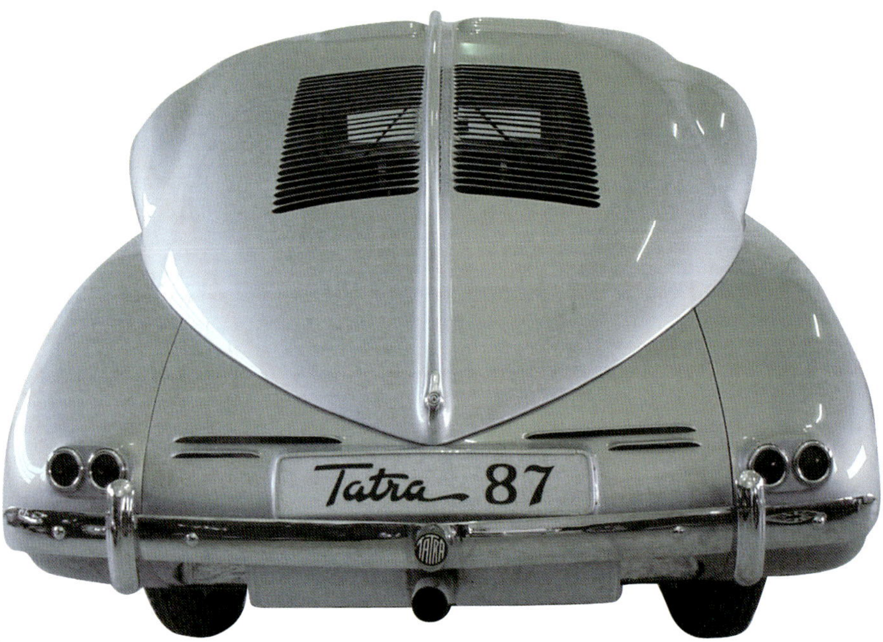

Hans (Nick) Roericht, **Hotelstapelgeschirr ›TC 100‹**
Stacking hotel crockery "TC 100", 1959

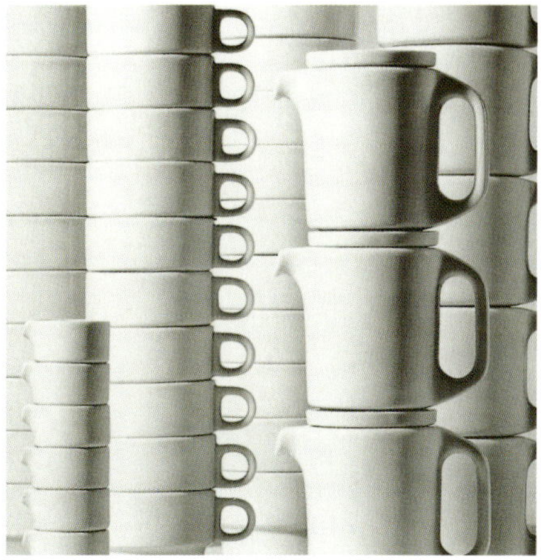

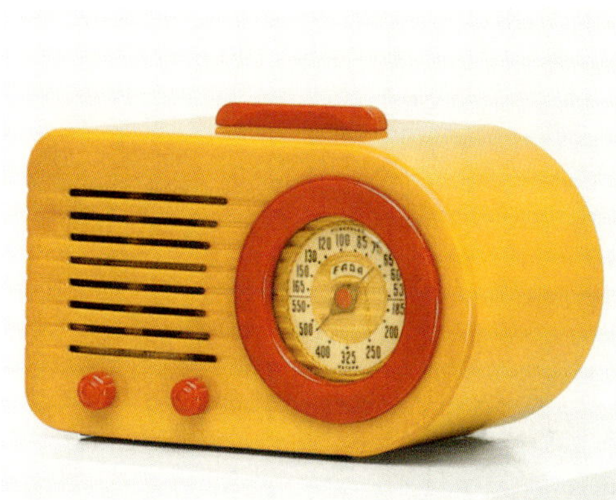

Radio ›Streamliner‹, Werksentwurf design prototype, 1940/45

Sony Design, **Unterhaltungsroboter ›AIBO ERS-111‹**
Entertainment robot "AIBO ERS-111", 1999

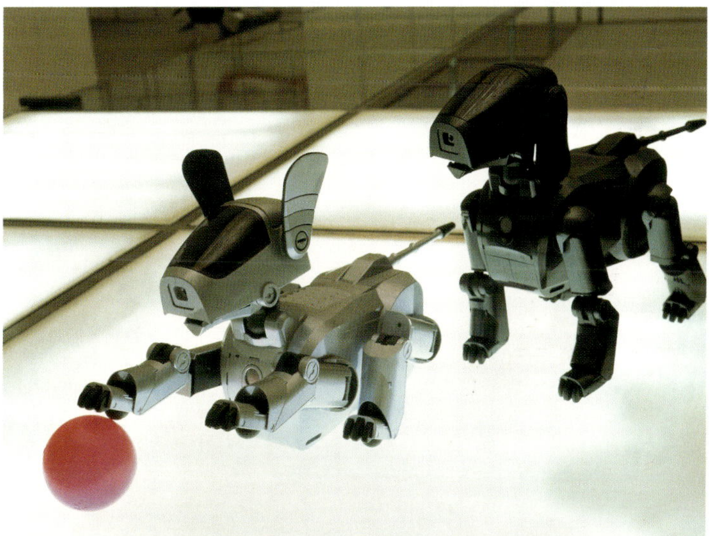

Architekturmuseum der Technischen Universität München

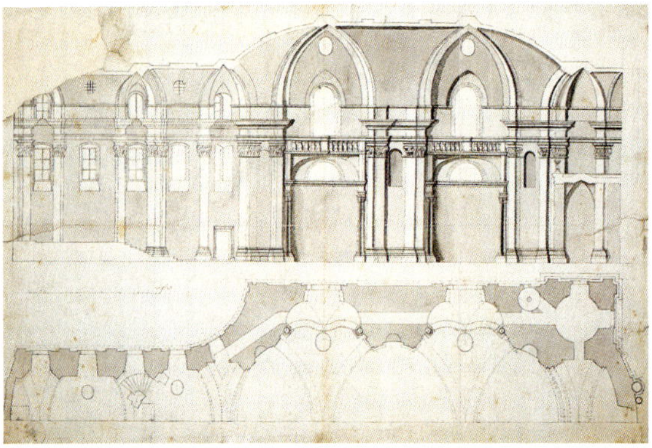

Johann Georg Dientzenhofer, **Klosterkirche Banz**
Banz Church, Längsschnitt und halber Grundriss
longitudinal section and partial floor plan,
um c. 1710

Das Architekturmuseum der Technischen Universität München zeigt wechselnde Ausstellungen in den nach Norden gerichteten Erdgeschossräumen der Pinakothek der Moderne. Die bedeutende Sammlung von Architekturzeichnungen, Fotografien und Modellen, die international zu den umfangreichsten ihrer Art gehört, hatte sich ursprünglich aus einem im 19. Jahrhundert angelegten Lehrkompendium mit Architekturzeichnungen, Plänen und Vorlageblättern entwickelt. In der Folge erweiterte sich die Sammlung durch umfangreiche Schenkungen und Ankäufe von Architekten- und Künstlernachlässen wie auch durch die Übernahme von Archiven zu einem bedeutenden wissenschaftlichen Archiv für Architekten, Architekturhistoriker und Denkmalpfleger. Die Bestände des Museums, das seit dem Zweiten Weltkrieg keine eigenen Ausstellungsräume mehr hatte, waren bislang in Depots untergebracht, jedoch wurden regelmäßig Ausstellungen in anderen Museen organisiert. Die Pinakothek der Moderne bietet dem Architekturmuseum nun insgesamt 600 Quadratmeter Ausstellungsfläche, auf der wichtige Positionen der Architekturgeschichte, einzelne Architektenpersönlichkeiten ebenso wie verschiedene Aspekte und Tendenzen der zeitgenössischen Architektur vorgestellt werden.

The Architekturmuseum der Technischen Universität München presents temporary exhibitions in the north-facing ground-floor rooms of the Pinakothek der Moderne. This important collection of architectural drawings, photographs and models is one of the largest of its kind in the world. Originally founded as a teaching and research compendium comprising architectural drawings and plans, it developed and grew from there, with donations, bequests and purchases from the estates of architects and artists, and the incorporation of archives, eventually becoming a significant archival facility for architects, architecture historians and conservationists. The museum's holdings have had no exhibition space of their own since the Second World War and have been kept in depots, being shown intermittently at other exhibition venues. The Pinakothek der Moderne now provides the collection with 600 square metres of exhibition space to present major positions and trends in architectural history, individual architects and various aspects of contemporary architecture.

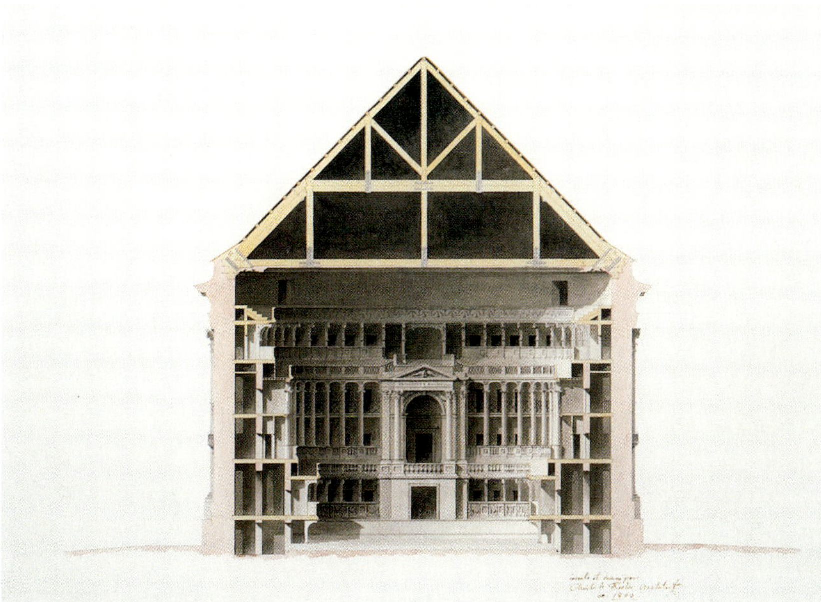

Carl von Fischer, **Entwurf für ein Opernhaus in Wien** Proposal for an opera house in Vienna, 1803

Karl Friedrich Schinkel, **Projekt des königlichen Schlosses auf der Akropolis in Athen** Project for a royal palace on the Athenian Acropolis, 1834

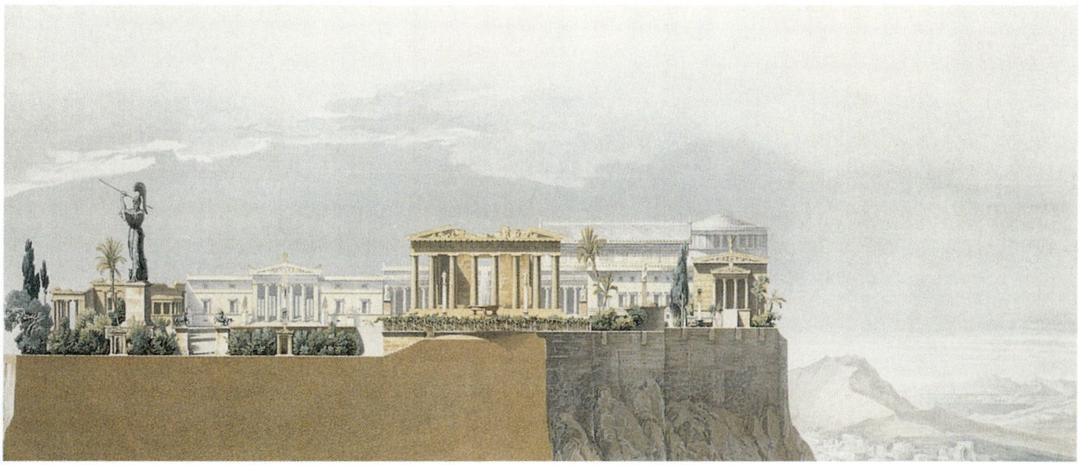

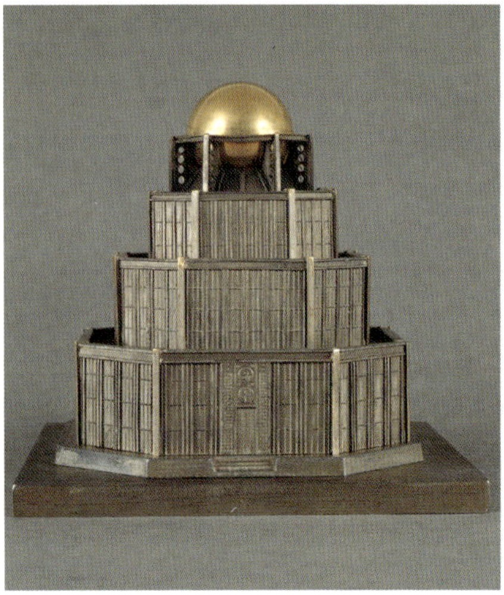

Bruno Taut/Franz Hoffmann, **Monument des Eisens auf der Internationalen Baufachausstellung Leipzig 1913** **Monument of Iron for the International Building Exhibition, Leipzig, 1913,** Modell model, um c. 1912/13

Vladimir G. Šuchov, **Šabolovka Radioturm** **Šabolovka radio tower,** Modell model, 2002

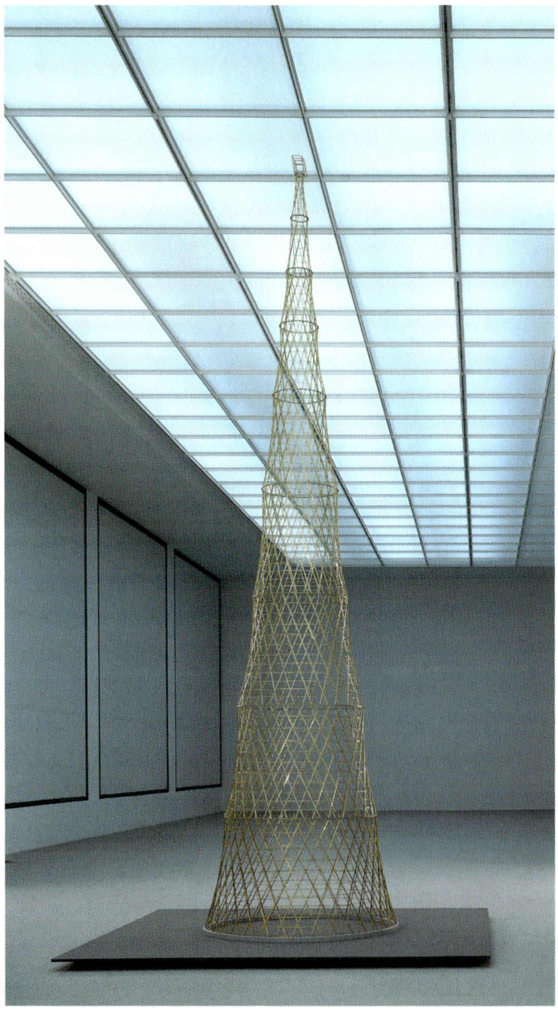

Erik Gunnar Asplund, **Pavillon für die Stockholmer Ausstellung 1930** **Pavilion for the Stockholm Exhibition, 1930,** um c. 1929/30

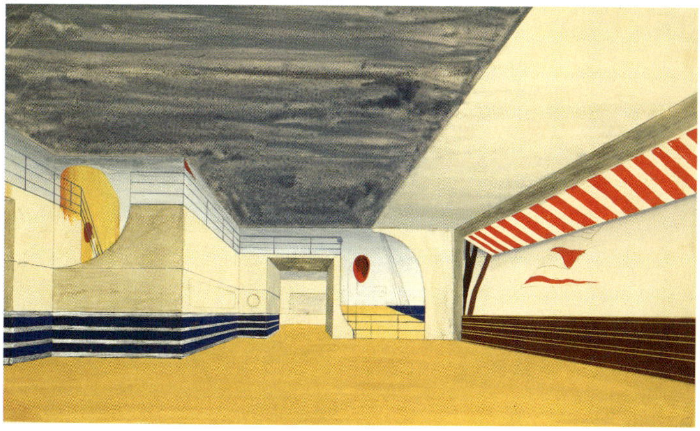

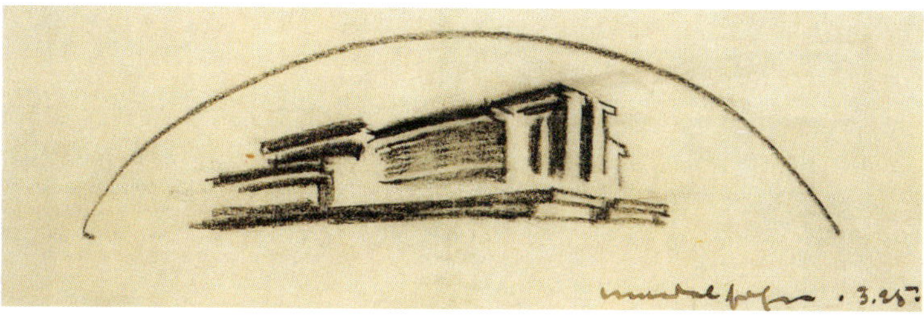

Erich Mendelsohn, **Haus Aron** **Aron House**, Entwurfszeichnung design drawing, 1925

Peter Zumthor, **Entwurf zu einem Hotel in Tschlin/Schweiz** **Proposal for a hotel in Tschlin, Switzerland**, Modell model, 2000

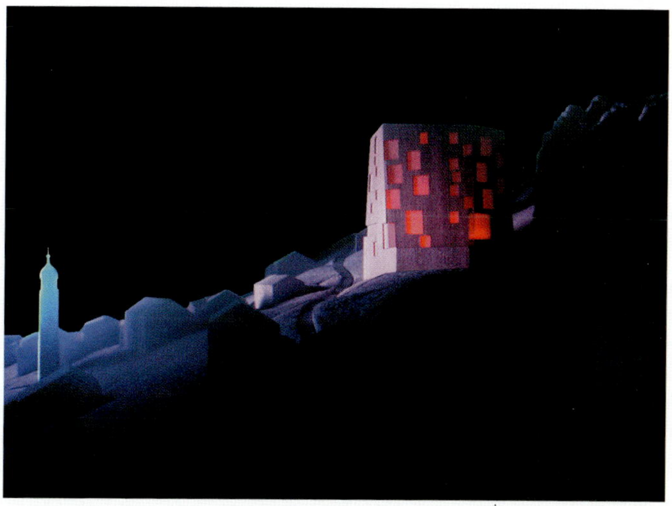

Stephan Braunfels, Dipl. Ing. Architekt BDA

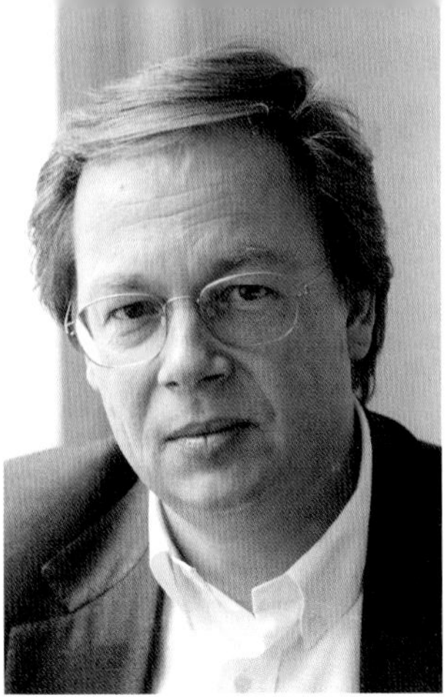

Foto: Uwe Rau

1950 Born in Überlingen/Lake Constance

1970–75 Studies architecture at the Technical University in Munich

Since 1978 Architectural office in Munich

1984 General urban design concept for the Hofgarten site in Munich

1987 Exhibits "Designs for Munich" at the German Architecture Museum in Frankfurt am Main

First prize in the competition to redesign the Marienhof in Munich

1991–93 Consultant to the City of Dresden

Guideline for the restoration of the inner city

1992 General urban design concept for the Altstadt Ring in Dresden

First prize in the competition to design the Museums of the 20th Century, located on the site of the former Türken Barracks in Munich

1993 First prize in the urban design competition for Georgplatz in Dresden

1994 First prize in the competition to design the German Parliament buildings (Alsenblock) in Berlin

First prize in the competition to redesign the Schloss Wilhelmshöhe Museum in Kassel

German Critics Prize 1994

Since 1996 Development plan for the Altstadt Ring in Dresden

Opens architectural office in Berlin

1998–2001 Construction of the Schloss Wilhelmshöhe Museum in Kassel

1996–2002 Construction of the Pinakothek der Moderne in Munich

Construction of the Paul-Löbe-Haus (Alsenblock) for the German Parliament in Berlin

1998–2003 Construction of the Marie-Elisabeth-Lüders-Haus (Luisenblock) in Berlin

1950 Geboren in Überlingen/Bodensee

1970–1975 Studium der Architektur an der Technischen Universität München

Seit 1978 Architekturbüro in München

1984 Städtebauliches Gesamtkonzept Hofgartenareal in München

1987 Ausstellung im Deutschen Architekturmuseum in Frankfurt am Main »Entwürfe für München«

1. Preis im städtebaulichen Realisierungswettbewerb für die Neugestaltung des Marienhofs in München

1991–1993 Berater der Landeshauptstadt Dresden

Leitbild für den Wiederaufbau der Innenstadt

1992 Städtebauliches Gesamtkonzept Altstadtring Dresden

1. Preis im Wettbewerb für die Museen des 20. Jahrhunderts auf dem Gelände der ehemaligen Türkenkaserne in München

1993 1. Preis im städtebaulichen Wettbewerb Georgplatz in Dresden

1994 1. Preis im Wettbewerb Bundestagsabgeordnetenhaus Alsenblock in Berlin

1. Preis im Wettbewerb Neugestaltung Museum Schloss Wilhelmshöhe in Kassel

Deutscher Kritikerpreis 1994

Seit 1996 Bebauungsplan für den Altstadtring Dresden

Architekturbüro in Berlin

1998–2001 Bau des Museums Schloss Wilhelmshöhe in Kassel

1996–2002 Bau der Pinakothek der Moderne in München

Bau des Paul-Löbe-Hauses (Alsenblock) für den Deutschen Bundestag in Berlin

1998–2003 Bau des Marie-Elisabeth-Lüders-Hauses (Luisenblock) für den Deutschen Bundestag in Berlin